George Hudson of York

60p.

Adulation

"Why is old York like New York?—Because in both 'The Hudson' facilitates commercial communication, and has established power and wealth."

Yorkshire Gazette, 1845

"I feel I should be safe were I to risk my existence on the honour and honesty of George Hudson . . . if ever I set my eyes on a man—and I have had some experience—whose manly port, physiognamy, and whole bearing characterised *an honest man*, a man superior to all meanness, it is George Hudson! A man I am proud to call my friend."

William Etty, April 1849

Execration

Do the tradesmen of York recollect how, . . . every man was marked out for persecution and exclusive dealing who dared to come between Mr. Hudson and "the wind of his nobility."

Yorkshireman, 1849

Exhortation

"Hudson come back, all is forgiven."

York and County, 1968

". . . there is no doubt that George Hudson brought to the City a lasting and important place in the life of the railways of this country . . . we should make an end to his disgrace . . ."

York Civic Trust Annual Report,
1969-70

George Hudson
of York

by

A.J.Peacock and David Joy.

Dalesman Books

1971

The Dalesman Publishing Company, Ltd.
Clapham (via Lancaster), Yorkshire
First published 1971
© A. J .Peacock and David Joy, 1971

ISBN: 0 85206 126 9

A. J. Peacock read Politics and Economics at Ruskin College, Oxford, from 1952-54, and graduated from Southampton University in 1957 with a history honours degree. He later received his MA for a study of land reform movements in Britain in the 19th century. He has written several works on working class movements, and is at present undertaking a social and political history of York in the first half of the 19th century. From this arose the interest in George Hudson. A. J. Peacock has been warden of the York Educational Settlement since 1960 and is a J.P. in York.

David Joy was educated at St. Peter's School, York, and worked in the city as a journalist until 1965. He has researched widely into the social and economic history of railways in the North, and has written, broadcast and lectured on this subject. He is at present working on a standard history of West Riding railways, and a biography of David Joy, the 19th century engineer and innovator.

Printed and Bound in Great Britain by
Galava Printing Co., Ltd., Hallam Road, Nelson, Lancashire

Contents

Illustrations are on pages 49–56 and 73–80; all unacknowledged pictures are from the authors' collections. The front cover shows:— Left: "Off the Rail,'. Leech's cartoon in *Punch* of Hudson's fall in 1849; right: An oil painting of Hudson, executed by I. Andrews in 1845 and now in the possession of Mr' Henry Hudson of York. The back cover depicts an election card produced by the Railway King when he stood as M.P. for Sunderland in 1845. The title page drawing, showing Hudson's effigy being removed from Madame Tussaud's waxworks for melting down, and the drawings on pages 7 and 84 are from *Punch*.

THIS is not a biography of George Hudson. Richard S. Lambert's work, *The Railway King*, first published in 1934, must—despite its inaccuracies—remain the standard introduction to the subject. Rather is it an attempt to penetrate the Hudson myth and examine in detail the background to his corruption and downfall. The first and major part of the book accordingly studies political movements in York in the 1830s and '40s, and the way in which they increasingly came under Hudson's dictatorship. For, unquestionably, Hudson's activities in York provide a vital clue to an understanding of his pyschologically rather puzzling railway career. The second part of the book looks at another intriguing question: how would Britain's railways have developed had there been no George Hudson.

ACKNOWLEDGEMENTS

Most of the quotations used are taken from the files of one or other of the York newspapers. The Howsham Poor Law Book is in the possession of the Rev. H. Fall, while Mrs. Frankie Beechey made the search of York Methodist records referred to. My good friend John Richardson of the Law Department of the University of Hull provided the legal comments on the Bottrill will, and the quote from the journal of Mary Backhouse Ecroyd is taken from a MSS work on *The Backhouse Family of Darlington* by Mr. F. Watson. The Brontë letters are printed in the *Proceedings of the Brontë Society*. The details of the amount of compensation received by Thomas Backhouse, when the first railway station in York was built on property hitherto occupied by him, are from a document in the British Transport Commission's archives at York, and other source materials used are in collections at the York Minister Library and the York City Library. My grateful thanks are due to all the people mentioned above, to Mrs. Sylvia Blanshard, who typed the script, and especially to Mr. Maurice Smith of the York City Library, and his two colleagues, Miss. Naomi Walls and Miss Jeanne Baxter, for their unfailing assistance to a persistent and perhaps tiresome customer.
A. J. Peacock. York Educational Settlement.
September 1971.

I am especially grateful to Mr K. Hoole for checking the chronology of Hudson's railway career, and to Mr. M. J. MacDonald (Keeper of Records, British Transport Historical Records, York) for help with illustrations. I owe a special debt to Mr. Henry Hudson of York for allowing me to photograph the painting of the Railway King and other material in his possession. York City Libraries and the Railway Museum, York, have also been most generous in their assistance.
David Joy. Hebden, Skipton.
October 1971.

Part One

"The Spouter of Fustian"

KING HUDSON'S LEVEE

GEORGE HUDSON was one of the most extraordinary men of the nineteenth century and certainly the most extraordinary man in York's modern history. Rising from comparitive obscurity, he became the most discussed, sought after, fawned over, and then the most vilified personage of his time—all within the space of twenty years. Now the attitude to the erstwhile "Railway King" seems to have gone a full circle. In the city in which he lived in the years of his predominance, in the city which he ruled over as rudely, as harshly, and as unscrupulously as any Tammany Hall boss, attempts are being made to "rehabilitate" him. Those attempts are based on certain contentions about him and his achievements as a railwayman. His rehabilitators however take no account of Hudson as a local politician. They take no account of what his rule meant to anyone who was not a member of the "Hudson Circus." Perhaps that is because this part of his career has so far not been studied in detail. This essay is an attempt to remedy that defect and, if it does, it will be seen that the historical analogies with Hudson have to be looked for among the Horatio Bottomleys, the Boss Tweeds and the Huey Longs, the shady financial manipulators and the unscrupulous party bosses.

The Hudson apologists, it is only fair to note, do not deny the dubious financial dealings that Hudson was proved to have perpetrated. They contend that whatever he may have done, whatever means of influencing men and companies he may have used, however much many of his colleagues (who perhaps deserved no better) may have suffered, all is outweighed by the legacy he left to "Old Ebor." George Hudson laid the basis for York's future prosperity, so the argument runs, by making it a great railway centre. In an oft-quoted phrase (that first seems to have been mentioned in 1922, in a book of reminiscences by a well-known writer on Yorkshire folk lore), he was said to have set out the objectives that motivated his whole career, which were achieved, and for which posterity owes him a dept of gratitude:

> ". . . in the early days of his career . . . when they were discussing the lines of country [sic] on the map through which the projected railways were to pass, Hudson called out in broad native accents, 'Mak all t' railways cum ti York'; which thing they did."

The phrase was taken over by Hudson's biographer, incorporated in the play *Sounding Brass*, and has been repeated *ad nauseam* in scores of books, sketches and articles. But Hudson did *not* make all the railways go to York, and neither was he the great innovator that is presupposed whenever the remark is quoted. York's businessmen were quick off the mark to get a line into their city, it is true, but Hudson was only one among many—and not the most important at that, according to one of his lackeys. Furthermore, they were acting strictly in accordance with earlier beliefs about what was necessary to relieve the city of the malaise that had overcome it at the the end of the eighteenth century. The second line, which really *did* make York a rail centre, owed nothing whatsoever to Hudson, and another was conceived originally by a competitor. Lastly, and this is practically ignored by his admirers, far from making what was ultimately the most important line of all go to York, Hudson did his utmost to stop it!

There is another part of the Hudson myth, and it is a part which was sedulously nurtured by Hudson himself, when it suited him, and was taken over by his biographer R.S. Lambert, then editor of *The Listener*, and author of that extraordinary book *The Haunting of Cashen's Gap*. According to this, Hudson was the poor boy who made good, the product of the self-help that Samuel Smiles made into one of the Victorians' greatest virtues. He "came to the city almost without a friend," he told the Corporation in 1838, "and with little in his pocket." In fact he had come under a cloud from a wealthy farming family. Lambert said he was from a humble family which he left "in straitened circumstances." In fact, his father left a large sum of money and had been High Constable for the division of Buckrose, Yorkshire.

George Hudson was born in 1800 in Howsham in the East Riding of Yorkshire. He was fifth son of John Hudson who died leaving an alleged fortune of £10,000 when the future Railway King was eight. His farms were divided up among his elder sons, one of whom replaced him as High Constable. The Howsham Poor Book, for the period 6 April 1815 to 6 April 1816, contains an entry saying, "Received of George Hudson for Bastardy . . . 12s 6d," and this may have had more than a little to do with his being sent to York.

Hudson was apprenticed to Nicholson and Bell, drapers and silk mercers of College Street, York. Six years later, when he was 21, George married Elizabeth, Nicholson's daughter, and became a partner in the firm. According to Lambert he was at one time a a Methodist class leader in the city, but a search of Methodist records has not substantiated this claim. Hudson was a Church and King Tory of ultra views for the whole of his career. "No Popery" and "Protection" were the two cardinal principles of his political creed.

In 1827 the first hints of shady dealings by George Hudson were heard. Lambert tells the story briefly, but without evidence for or against. In that year, so the story goes, Hudson's great uncle Matthew Bottrill* died, leaving George a fortune of £30,000 and making him one of the richest men in York. Contemporaries noted that young Hudson had hardly left the old man's bedside during his last illness, and drew very unpleasant conclusions from the fact that Bottrill's

---

Lambert calls him William on one occasion he mentions him and Matthew on the other.

will was altered during his last days. Years later the *Yorkshireman*, when the Railway King was in disgrace, produced a pamphlet in which the affair was mentioned again. Legal action against Hudson was considered, it alleged. "Certain it is, that Mr. Botterill [sic] altered his will while on his death-bed, and that Mr. Hudson was his constant companion during his latter hours." A study of the Bottrill will suggests that there is a *prima facie* case against Hudson. It is impossible however to say exactly to what extent he benefited.

Matthew Bottrill is described in a York City guide of 1823 as a "gentleman" with an address in Monkgate. In 1807 he voted in the great Yorkshire election, qualifying to do so through a freehold at Newton-on-Derwent, and giving his support to William Wilberforce. It is quite true that he altered his will shortly before his death. The old man died on 25 May, and the will is dated 21 April. "George Hudson of the City of York, Mercer" was named as sole executor. By the terms of the will, Matthew's brothers and several servants received annuities varying from £20 to £50 a year. £500 each was given to several nieces and nephews, and the total legacies came to £4,500. All Matthew's "lands tenements and Real Estate situate at Osbaldwick and Huntington," however, were left to his "great nephew George Hudson of Goodramgate." Probate was sworn at under £10,000, which means that Hudson as residuary beneficiary could have received something in excess of £5,000 personalty. But the valuation of £10,000 would be limited to personalty alone. The value of the land at Osbaldwick, Huntington and *maybe elsewhere* would not be included for probate since realty passed directly to the heir or devisee, and this remained so until 1897. Bottrill owned property at Newton-on-Derwent in 1807, as has been shown. What he had elsewhere will probably never be known. The future Railway King may or may not have received as much as contemporaries thought—he may even have received more. The story that the old man left money or property to others of the Hudson family, however is obviously false. No Hudson other than George and his son are mentioned.

So by the late 1820s George Hudson was rich and he became an important man in the political life of York. In 1829 the Tory party split over the issue of Catholic Emancipation and the Whigs seized their opportunity. General elections took place in 1830 and 1832 and parliamentary reform ensued. The electorate was widened and a step in the direction of democracy was taken. But men still voted openly—the secret ballot was a half a century away. While the old system of voting remained, there also remained gross bribery and corruption. George Hudson was to be disburser in chief for the York Tory party for many years.

York was a Whig city. It was dominated by a closed Whig Corporation, which was often presided over by a member of one of the great Whig families of Fitzwilliam or Dundas. It was represented in

Parliament by two members, but representation was usually split between the Tories and the Whigs. The former could not break into the seat of municipal power, but at election times representation went to those who spent most. Tory gold usually procured one seat. (Sir Mark Masterman Sykes, the "Blue Baronet," was said to have doubled the price of a vote in 1807 and established a norm for years to come). Only in very exceptional times, like 1832, was one or other of the parties able to seize both seats.

The Whig governments of the early 1830s were among the great reforming governments of the nineteenth century. But some of their reforms, notably that of the Poor Law, cost them dear. Their refusal to extend the vote beyond the middle class, and their treatment of the agricultural labourers of Dorset, alienated the working class. The new Poor Law was detested and violently resisted. The Tory party, or many of its most prominent members, joined forces with mill workers and labourers, to stop its introduction in many parts of the country. In a few short years all the goodwill of the Reform Bill struggle had been dissipated. In 1835 a general election took place, and George Hudson took part in a sensational contest in York.

Things were going well for the Tories and they were helped in York by the unpopularity of one of the Whig members. This was E.R. Petre, the first Catholic Lord Mayor of the City, and someone who had not paid for the votes he had received in 1832. Petre was the first declared candidate, followed very quickly by John Henry Lowther of Swillington. Lowther, a nephew of the Earl of Lonsdale, was a Tory who had been first approached, unsuccessfully, to stand for York in 1826 as a candidate "friendly to the Constitution, and decidedly opposed to . . . concessions to the Roman Catholics." He had sat for Cockermouth (1816-26), then for Wigton (1826-30) and then for Cockermouth again. In 1832, however, he stood for the first time in York. At his selection committee meeting (in August 1832) his nomination had been proposed by John Blanchard, and seconded by George Hudson. Lowther failed to get in, however, despite massive bribery. In the heady atmosphere of the Reform Bill struggle, men actually voted for nothing. It was not to happen very often.

Lowther and Petre (who eventually withdrew) were joined as candidates in 1835 by Charles Francis Barkley and J.C. Dundas, both Whigs, and the contest got under way. The electorate in those days consisted of the freemen of the city (whom the Whigs had wanted to disenfranchise in 1832) resident within seven miles of the city, and the £10 house-holders enfranchised in 1832. Each had two votes and the parties solicited "plumpers" (one vote cast for one candidate only) or "split votes," which on this occasion only the Whigs would ask for, for obvious reasons. Payment was always delayed until after the last date on which a petition alleging corruption could be laid before Parliament.

At this election the Tories attacked the Whigs because of the Poor Law (George Hudson was actually in favour of it—the only occasion on which he departed from a solid, unwavering support of his party); presented themselves as "the freeman's friends" (they claimed credit for defeating the attempts to end the freeman's vote); and presented themselves, also, as reformers, most of them taking their stand on Sir Robert Peel's manifesto in which he accepted the finality of the reform measures of 1832. The canvass took 20 days, which the Whigs said gave their opponents too much time "to nobble the electorate" (nearly 3,000 in number in 1835). On 5 January the hustings were held in St. Sampson's Square.

The hustings took place a day before polling began, and on this occasion the polling was spread over two days. (Some electors held back as long as possible—"the Waiters on Providence" one candidate called them—to put up the price of their votes, but the danger of this proceeding was that one man might concede defeat, bring the contest to an early close to save himself money, and the voter would get nothing). The Lord Mayor presided over the hustings and called for nominations and seconders. Having been proposed, the candidates then addressed the crowds and an election by a show of hands was demanded. The Mayor then declared the two successful contenders, whereupon those defeated would demand a poll. This commenced the following day, at booths placed at six different positions in the city. Lowther's procession to the hustings had had in it "a coal sack decorated with dark blue rosettes, and most expressive of that most orthodox sentiment of Toryism that every man has his *price*, from the bribe of a met of coals to the more *sovereign* reason prefigured by the *gold* lettered standards which followed," lamented a Whig paper, "gold and drunkeness," it said, "prevailed over reason, moral principle, and the most virtuous and powerful arguments." C.F. Barkley said that 200 of his promised voters had plumped for the Tory. The *Yorkshireman* said that "gold alone turned the scale," and took Lowther to the top of the poll. The *York Courant* called the election "discreditable" to the city. " . . . where is the morality, the common decency of those brawlers for the altar and throne," it asked,

"in bringing up their *hired voter*, reeling from the dram-shop, to hiccup forth the bribery oath, and perjure themselves in the face of their neighbours! Where is the morality of bringing to the poll, men—we almost repudiated the term, when applied to such in a state—of beastly intoxication, to exercise one of the most solemn and important rights of freemen! Carriages, too, which even in the old corrupt No-Popery days of Toryism, were only employed to bring up the halt and the sick, have now been kept in constant requisition, to carry the healthy and the strong, except they might be incapacitated by inebriation, some two or three hundred yards from their revelling rendezvous to the Poll."

Some electors, like the tenants of the Earl de Grey at Clifton, were told how to vote. Those with some degree of freedom of action were persuaded by booze and bribes. At the declaration of the poll (Lowther—1,499; Dundas—1,301; Barkley—919), J.C. Dundas hinted that there would be an enquiry into the election—465 people who had promised him plumped for Lowther, he maintained. What appears to have shocked him and his colleagues was not so much the bribery, as the extent of it. A Select Committee of the House of Commons eventually investigated what went on in 1835 (and to some extent 1832 also). One of the star witnesses was George Hudson who hedged and shifted before his interrogators as Frank Costello did when, years later, he appeared before a Senate enquiry, pleading the fifth amendment and unable to "charge" his memory when it suited him.

Barkley was the more radical of the two Whig candidates of 1835 and a believer in "purity of election" (he only spent £300 on his campaign). Two petitions went to Parliament from York asking for an enquiry. The first started from the York Society for the Diffusion of Political Knowledge, a radical society that owed much to Barkley's initiative and a member of which was a young solicitor called George Leeman. The second petition emanated from the city's Quaker community, shocked at the drunkeness and brawling that were the inevitable accompaniment of any York election. Samuel Tuke, John Clemesha, Thomas Backhouse and Joseph Rowntree the elder were among the petitioners. So, too, were a few people who, in later years, paid court to the Railway King, and who ignored the things then that they found so objectionable in 1835. James Chadwick was one. Chadwick was to become a long-serving Tory councillor in the Hudson years, Lord Mayor and then one of those who viciously turned on his erstwhile leader when the chips were down.

The minutes and evidence of the Select Committee on the election of 1835 are essential reading for anyone interested in the techniques of political campaigning in York in the nineteenth century. George Hudson was by this time a man of substance, and treasurer of what should be now called the Conservative party. The committee heard that Lowther, with an eye to the future, had £3 paid for a plumper in 1832—when he had *no* chance of success! Three years later, as soon as he thought the coast was clear, Hudson distributed the "golden ointment" through the post. "We think it a much better plan to let them have the money at their own houses, than take them from their work and pay them at a public-house," Hudson told John Moxon, one of the witnesses. Hudson, an early witness, anxious not to "criminate" himself, was helped by a poor memory. His wife had been active at canvassing and commanding votes, and the committee heard of dozens of incidents of "personating" voters, violence, intimidation and drunkeness. James Balwick was a Lowther voter whose story was elicited in cross-examination:

2266   What impresses his case upon your mind?—He came very tipsy; they
       did not think him at all fit to vote; the bribery oath was put to him,
       and he could not understand what they said; he kept muttering and
       making a noise, and they did not think him fit to vote.
2267   Who thought that?—The deputy Sheriff; and we had a great deal to do,
       we persuaded him to go away till he was in a more proper state.
2268   Did he come again?—Yes.
2269   Who brought him?—Mr. Lowther came with him.
2270   How long afterwards?—It might be half-an-hour.
2271   What did Mr. Lowther do?—He urged him to take his vote, and
       thought he was in a proper state.
2272   Was he admitted?—Yes.
2273   How did he poll?—He polled for Mr. Lowther
2274   A plumper?—Yes.

The price of a plumper, at least for a time, was still £3 it was established.

The Select Committee led to nothing. The Whigs had miscalculated. They, too, were shown to have bribed—although only in
retaliation they maintained—and they certainly did not do so on
the scale that Hudson and his colleagues did. Lowther was not
unseated, and York continued to return two members for the rest
of Hudson's life and long afterwards.

By 1835 then, George Hudson, "the spouter of fustian" his
enemies called him, had risen to prominence in the political life of
York, presiding over the Conservative party machine with considerable skill at election times. (There were then no permanent party
political organisations). A manipulator and a briber Hudson
certainly was, but it would be wrong to present him as anything
unique. Hudson was a briber and a manipulator in an age when a
vote was regarded as a negotiable asset. He eventually used the
techniques of parliamentary elections to fix municipal contests.
When he used the same methods in business—and when the dividends
went down—the writing was on the wall.

GEORGE HUDSON advanced to prominence in the city of
York through the Conservative party, but the avenues to real
power were closed to people like him until the end of 1835.
York was governed by a closed corporation almost entirely com-
posed of Whigs, self-elected, and self-perpetuating. The only time
Tories got into it was when they were punished by their opponents
and elected (like Robert Cattle) to fill the incredibly expensive
office of Sheriff, and accepted rather than pay the fine for not doing
so. In 1835 all this was altered and Hudson was given his great
opportunity—as a result of a Whig reform.

In this year the system of municipal government in the large towns was amended. Most were controlled by closed Tory corporations who used corporation funds and power to influence elections. (The Whigs did so in York it is quite clear—at each election in the old days one Whig candidate was recognised to be a corporation nominee— but how exactly the influence was used it is difficult to determine, except over vulnerable people like the tenants of municipal property and so on).

The reformers wanted to break control by closed corporations and an investigation into municipal government was instigated. The hearing before the commissioners who visited York elicited detailed descriptions of how the old system worked at the end of its life. Hudson appeared before it and gave evidence about policing the city. Eventually a Bill was prepared which had a stormy passage through Parliament, largely because the Whigs tried again to graft on to it a clause disenfranchising the freemen at parliamentary elections. Altered considerably, it completed its course through Parliament and municipal government was reformed. The reformers at large were to have an opportunity of seizing control of the big towns. In York the conservatives were to have *their* chance of ending the Whig monopoly. The first elections were arranged for December 1835.

Under the municipal reform measures, York was divided into six (as against the four ancient) wards. Each of these wards was to be represented by six councillors, for whom there was a property qualification. Initially the councillors were to sit for either one, two or three years (depending on their position in the poll) and thereafter for three years. The annual elections were to be held in November of each year and the electorate was to consist of £10 householders (no freemen). Each year a burgess list was to be produced which was to be open to objection or alteration. The annual revising courts (there was one on the parliamentary list also) were to prove a great fillip to party organisation and provide much work for solicitors like George Leeman, a Liberal, and Hewley Graham, a Conservative.

The Conservatives took to municipal electioneering with tremendous enthusiasm, working secretly, producing a list of supported candidates ("their *select* list of their *elect*"), and engaging in an extensive canvass. The Liberals, as the ruling party should now be called, showed their traditional inertia, yet secured a majority. The Tories used all the usual methods of influencing electors and in Bootham obtained every seat. Elected for Monk ward (third in the poll under James Meek and Charles James Hanson) was "George Hudson, draper."

During the passage of the municipal reform bill through Parliament the Tory Lords, as a wrecking measure, had inserted into it provisions whereby aldermen, to sit for six years, were to be elected by the councillors themselves. (Initially half were to sit for only

three years). The Liberals prepared a list and 14 names went before
the corporation. At the first poll for the 12 seats ten Liberals were
elected and the last four candidates had an equal number of votes—
two Conservatives, two Liberals. Making a great show of tolerance,
on a second poll the Liberals allowed two Conservatives in. They were
Jonathan Gray, solicitor to the See of York, and George Hudson.
When the bye elections caused by the aldermanic elections (four
councillors were among the 12) and the refusals of some people
to serve had taken place, the Liberals had a clear majority of eight
(18 councillors and ten aldermen, to 18 councillors and two aldermen). Liberal inertia had allowed the Conservatives to pull back
from a much worse position. At those bye elections they took three
seats the Liberals had won earlier. A great use was made of the illib-
leral clauses 32 and 35 of the municipal reform act, the result of a
Tory amendment "ingeniously contrived to mar the efficiency of the
bill." These clauses ordered that all voting papers should be kept
and made available for inspection for a period of six months after
an election. The York Tories carried out a search, studied the re-
turns of December and used their information to effect:

> "many voters were pressingly canvassed, and some positively *commanded* to
> give their votes to Tory candidates at the second elections, who had voted
> exclusively in favour of the Liberal candidates at the first."

Like many latter-day political parties the York Tories were quick
to point out that although in a minority on the new Corporation,
they had in fact received more votes than their opponents. The
figures cast for the candidates who eventually made up the first
reformed corporation were 2,489 against 2,082. ". . . the new corporation of York, elected by the boasted system of popular suffrage,
is directly opposed to the majority of citizens who voted," moaned
the Tory *Gazette.* If this were so the new council should be attacked,
and attacked it was from the start.

The Liberals had no heart for municipal power, and had no
ability to organise the disparate elements that went to make up
their party. The draughtsmen responsible for the reform act had
completely forgotten to include provisions for managing the common
lands belonging to large boroughs, and the Tories whipped up the
freemen against the York Corporation on this issue. They never
tired of pointing out that, although the parties had an equal number
of councillors, the Liberals had seized 80 per cent of aldermanic
seats. The Tories were also in a position to render much of the
work of the council ineffective. Incredible though it seems, the
Liberals had sat back and allowed their opponents to obtain major-
ities on both the Finance and Watch Committees—and effectively
policing the city was one of the major tasks laid at the door of the
new corporation.

Alderman Hudson emerged as a tremendously effective party

boss, keeping party feeling high—indeed, stepping it up as the months went by. Charles James Hanson was a particular object of vitriolic attacks by him—being accused of voting illegally (he was Chief Constable for the Lower division of the City and Ainsty) and submitting a bill of £20 for collecting £200 in rates. The debate in which Hanson was put on trial must be one of the bitterest in York's municipal history. Robert Cattle, whose position as the city's leading Tory Hudson had usurped (and who desperately wanted to be an alderman), complained — disingenuously — of "the rancour and party feeling" which characterised the corporation's debates.

It was a bad year for the Liberals. They had chosen their candidates, initially, in a slap-happy fashion and there were few in their ranks below the leadership who could match the expertise of Hudson, Cattle and the others. They had allowed themselves to be outmanoeuvred over filling the Finance and Watch Committees and the Conservatives practically wrecked their schemes for policing the city. Hudson raised the cry of peculation, and prospects looked bad for the ruling party at the November elections of 1836.

Again the Conservatives made gains, and again they were the result of more efficient organising and more efficient bribing. Again both sides were not without blame. Robert Henry Anderson, a Liberal solicitor, a Roman Catholic and a long term contender for the highest municipal honours (more will be heard of him later) stood for Walmgate (and got in). Personating went on there, the *Gazette* said, false voting papers were sent out, and John Kyle (Liberal), who headed the poll, kept an open house:

> "it is notorious,—in fact it was palpable as the noon-day sun, — that treating was extensively resorted to. Spirits and beef were supplied in abundance. Mr. KYLE'S dramshop in the Pavement was in great request, his gin was said "to speak all languages", significant enough at least for the special inspiration it was intended to convey. And yet this person and MR. ANDERSON, two of the successful radical candidates for Walmgate, were conspicuous in . . . last year's Parliamentary inquiry into the alleged bribery, corruption, and drunkeness of the York Elections."

But Anderson and Kyle were exceptions. Most of the Liberals had deeper consciences and were unwilling to bribe. William Hargrove, editor of the *York Herald* and *York Courant*, and Oswald Allen, candidates for Monk, never bothered to canvass and were never officially adopted. As a result of the contests the Conservatives made considerable advances, winning eight out of the 12 seats contested. They now had a majority of councillors and municipal control by them seemed but a short way off. Their methods were described by various Liberals. For example, in Guildhall *The Punch Bowl* was the scene of tremendous treating and there Henry Bellerby got in. In Monk, where James Chadwick was returned, there was "beastly drunkeness." Everywhere, the *Courant* said, Hudson's colleagues "had recourse to those ancient Tory and very legitimate and honourable "appliances" . . . of sending your labourers into the *vineyard* at an early hour of the day and passing them off as the *double* of some honest voter, whom ye suspected would deliver himself of his burden at a later hour . . . and we have to add to all this, the secret intimidation,—the covertly offered *bribe*, even to the paying the individual's debts . . ." In Castlegate, George Leeman (who got in) said there was corruption "such as [was] unknown to the oldest inhabitants present." There the Tories had started another "professed reformer" themselves in an attempt to keep Leeman out, and a placard had gone round announcing that "The only safe way to throw Leeman overboard is to vote for [Edward] Gibson [the professed reformer] and [Benjamin] Crosby," the Conservative.

A year later 14 seats had to be filled (John Kyle had died and John Wolstenholme had been made an alderman). The vacancies represented an equal number of Liberal and Conservative seats, and Tory methods of electioneering were the usual ones of "solicitations of punch and trombones." In Monk, George Hudson presided over the poll and read out the names of each elector and whom he voted for—a proceeding which prompted the *Courant* angrily to demand the secret ballot. This time the Liberals were even more demoralised than before. In Bootham, the Tory ward *par excellence*, no candidates were put up at all, and in others only "feint" candidates were put in. There was no Liberal canvassing, no electioneering. To the Conservatives "money was no object," and the result was that they took ten of the 14 seats. There was now a Tory majority on the council of two (25 : 23) and the Hudson era was about to begin—a decade of unbroken Tory rule. ". . . the Whig-Radical party may bid adieu to that power which they so long wielded in the old close corporation," said the *Gazette*, "and which, by mere luck, they held for a short space of time under the new order of things."

In December 1835 after the first municipal (and aldermanic) elections the Liberals in York had had a large majority. By 1837 they were in a minority. They were out of power because of the effective campaigning and organising of their opponents, and the driving spirit behind them was George Hudson. The Liberals nationally were running out of steam, and their followers throughout the country were suffering because of the government's unpopularity. So things were going well for Hudson and his colleagues (at an election in 1837 Lowther beat Dundas into second place by a considerable margin), but great skill and energy had been shown by them in capitalising on their chances. By 1837 Hudson had been handling large numbers of men, and having things his own way for nearly five years. He had been a key figure in three general elections, and three municipal contests. Under him the Conservatives had pulled back from the devastation of 1832 and J.H. Lowther was securely ensconced at Westminster. Locally, Hudson and his associates had ended the

years in the wilderness for their party, and it had all, in the last resort, been bought. It was a heady draught Hudson had been taking
on board. Every man "had his *price*" was his belief, according to his
enemies, and they were right. ("Price" was a pun on the name of
Captain Price, a half-pay officer who, along with Cattle, had been
the real leader of the York Tories before Hudson).

Who was to be the first Conservative Lord Mayor of York? The
answer was obvious. In November 1837 Alderman George Hudson,
now described in the poll books and guides as "gentleman," took up
residence in the Mansion House. The Liberals had decided to give
their support to John Wolstenholme as first Tory Lord Mayor of
York, but Hudson was an automatic choice for his party. ". . . the
new Lord Mayor seemed to see in his term of office a grand opportunity to feast his way into the hearts of his fellow-citizens,
and . . . drown all discord and opposition in champagne and sherry."
The Mansion House became the scene of tremendous junketings.
Never had the city seen such ostentation. The inaugural civic banquet
was followed by tremendous celebrations on the Queen's birthday
and at the coronation. The poor were not entirely forgotten and on
coronation day Hudson organised a huge civic procession and meal,
at which 14,000 children and adults were admitted free. ". . . we
believe him calculated to become a popular Lord Mayor," said a
Whig paper when he was elected, and it was right. Hudson was
popular with everyone: those who were invited to his bean feasts,
the tradesmen who supplied him, and the poor who enjoyed his
flamboyance and the occasional handout. Everyone except the
Liberals.

The public at large saw Hudson the big spender. On the Corporation, Hudson—the party boss—personalised everything, riding
rough-shod over the effete opposition and keeping Leeman and the
more able Liberals off the main committees. During the year of his first
Mayoralty the question of the administration of the city charities
became a hot issue for, according to the Liberals, they were used
unashamedly for political ends— a man called Daniel, for example,
whose politics were "wrong" was refused assistance.

The way in which the Lord Mayor pursued his opponents might
be illustrated by his treatment of Robert Henry Anderson and
Charles Robinson. During the debates on the city charities, Anderson
was pilloried unmercifully. He was hated by the Tories because of
the part he had played in the 1835 election petition, and because of
his involvement in the trouble over the city charities. Immediately
after municipal reform, when the Liberals had control over the city,
new charity trustees had had to be appointed. The Liberals had
originally submitted a list of nominees in which the Quakers were
said to be over-represented. This drove Hudson, who loathed the
Society of Friends, into such a fury that he broke off instructing the
Gazette reporter on what to report, and launched into an incredibly

bitter attack on the Quakers. Instead of using their majority, the Liberals—true to form—allowed themselves to be outflanked, and permitted Hudson and his friends to pack the trustees and create a High Church-Tory monopoly.

At this stage Robert Henry Anderson was instructed by Joseph Parkes, a well-known Birmingham radical, to try to undo what had been done and to petition the Lord Chancellor under Clause 71 of the Municipal Corporations Act, asking him (a Whig) to override the council and appoint trustees himself. This Anderson did to the accompaniment of vitriolic attacks from the Hudsonians, who accused the Liberals of trying to do what they thought they had succeeded in doing for themselves—". . . to obtain within the grasp of their tools those charitable endowments intended for the poor freemen and their widows," that they might use them as "bribes amongst their dependants, in order to possess an undue influence over them, and deter them from giving conscientious votes."

Anderson was taunted with having attempted to make money out of the appeal to the Lord Chancellor, and in 1838 the council debated the question of the petition. Robert Henry had indeed submitted a bill of £73 and was accused of a "job," and in November was violently opposed when he was up for re-election to the council. Anderson's colleague for the representation of Castlegate was the Quaker, Thomas Backhouse, and both, the *York Chronicle* said, distributed drink on a grand scale. In retaliation they would have said, no doubt.

Charles Robinson had taken a prominent part in the debate on Anderson's expenses and was loathed by Hudson. Robinson, a druggist of Micklegate, had joined the council as a Liberal in 1836, and at each of the revisions of the municipal voters' lists had been harassed by the Tories on the grounds that he was not "an inhabitant householder." Robinson lived in a house in Micklegate, a part of which was let to a lodger. His qualifications stood while the Liberals controlled the city (and had a majority of the assessors), but in 1838, with Hudson himself presiding, it was decided that, as he had "not the exclusive right to the front door, he had no vote." By Clause 28 of the Reform Act a councillor had to be qualified as a burgess, and Hudson's decision meant that Robinson had to resign. In November a writ of mandamus was served on the Lord Mayor demanding Robinson's re-admission to the council, and later the case appeared in the Court of Queen's Bench (where it was dismissed). The *Gazette* gloated over Robinson's discomfiture in a jingle. (The William Peacock mentioned was the liberal assessor who went along with Hudson's decision):

> To the Court of Queen's Bench I foolishly go,
> To reverse the decision of Peacock and Co.;
> In *costs* I'm condemned after very short parley,
> Alas!! for the pocket of poor little Oh-ley."

Anderson and Robinson were but two among many who were learning what it meant to cross the Railway King.

In November 1838 an equal number of candidates from each party retired from the council and as a result of the elections of that year the Conservatives made a gain of one. Then six aldermen retired—Hudson and Cattle (who had replaced Jonathan Gray) and four Liberals. This time the Tories got their own back. A party list was prepared consisting of five Conservatives (Hudson, Cattle, John Swann, William Matterson and W. Stephenson Clark) and one Liberal who was sympathetic to Hudson. The timing of those aldermanic elections of 1838 was to become of crucial importance in a prolonged legal squabble.

Having elected their new aldermen, the Council turned to choosing the Lord Mayor. The Liberals optimistically put forward the name of Alderman Thomas Gregory but the Conservatives put up Hudson again. The sycophancy with which the move was greeted is incredible. John Roper, Tory councillor for Guildhall, a brewer, said that "He knew the tradesmen of York look forward anxiously to [Hudson's] reappointment", and the great man assured his hearers that the tradesmen *would* indeed benefit. Whereas James Meek, one of the leading Liberals, spent his money on building Methodist chapels, Hudson said he spent his on lavish entertainments. James Richardson, Conservative, solicitor and councillor for Bootham Ward, outdid everyone in buttering up to Hudson. ". . . in my voting paper," he said, "I shall insert the words—'I vote for George Hudson, Esq., as Mayor, and against Thomas Gregory, Esq., as Mayor, and I recommend all my friends to do the same.'" Richardson was to become a very important member of the Hudson circus.

The Liberals were furious at the choice of Hudson as Lord Mayor for a second term. They contended that, as his term of office as an alderman had ended, he had not been eligible. The election of a Lord Mayor should have been first business of the council, they maintained, but the aldermanic elections had taken place beforehand. The *Yorkshireman*, the city's radical newspaper, week after week produced evidence to prove that the Tories had acted *ultra vires*. George Hicks Seymour, Leeman, the harassed Robinson and Charles Poppleton, the linen manufacturer of Osbaldwick, and Liberal councillor for Walmgate, met and decided to raise funds to try the legality of what had happened in York. A public meeting was held and £100 was subscribed immediately to take the case to court. Affidavits were prepared, the *York Herald* said, "on which the application for a *quo warranto* [a Queen's Bench writ by which a person or persons were called upon to show by what warrant he or they held, claimed or exercised an office or franchise] will be founded." Seymour and Leeman were appointed solicitors, and it was announced on 17 November that "the Attorney General will be retained, and a rule *nisi* applied for next week."

In late January 1839 the case of the Queen versus Hudson came up in the Queen's Bench. Sir F. Pollock "showed cause against a rule for a quo warranto, calling upon George Hudson, Esq. to show by what authority he held the office of Lord Mayor in the city of York." The case however, was not decided until May 1840, when a decision was given in the Queen versus McGowan which also decided the issue in York. The proceedings of 9 November 1838 *were* declared contrary to law. Hudson was *not* legally Lord Mayor—but by now he had been out of office for six months! The *Yorkshireman* raised the question of the aldermen. Were they legally elected? And what was the position of the current Lord Mayor (William S. Clark) who had been chosen from them?

HUDSON was in control of his party in York and in control of the council; he was also becoming a big man in the railway world, and would be a big employer of labour. There is no doubt that his second term of office delighted him because it angered the Liberals, and underlined both the subservience of the city at large and the position of power and influence his money, his bribing and his organising ability had obtained for him. He was not without critics, but to all intents and purposes he would be eventually. The really great days were yet to come, although he had achieved enough to have satisfied many men by the time his second term of office ended. An extra reason for remaining Lord Mayor was that he wanted to be first magistrate when the railway was officially opened on 29 May 1839.

This was the York and North Midland, a line initially from York to South Milford, where a junction was made with the line from Leeds to Selby. The "Lowther" engine and tender left York shortly after one o'clock, and completed the round trip in under an hour and a half. The entertainments that followed were lavish even by Hudson's standards. "During the evening the Lady Mayoress gave a dance and supper at the Mansion House. The clerks dined at the Windmill, whilst the workmen were regaled at various places in the city through the liberality of the directors." At the Guildhall 200 gentlemen had begun to dine at half-past four and had not risen until ten. George Hudson and George Stephenson had presided.

The York and North Midland company had its origins in a meeting at *Tomlinson's Hotel* York in December 1833, where a group of businessmen including Hudson assembled under the chairmanship of James Meek, a wealthy currier, the Lord Mayor in the Liberals last year in power and the Wesleyan whom Hudson poked fun at for building chapels. (R.S. Lambert and Leslie Burgess, author of

Sounding Brass, confuse Meek with John Meek, coal merchant of Gillygate and later a Tory councillor. Lambert says that Meek was Sheriff of York in 1833 which is also incorrect).

The group at *Tomlinson's Hotel* had met to discuss the question of taking a railway into York and they have been represented as innovators, far-seeing businessmen undertaking a revolutionary step on behalf of their city. In fact, they were doing precisely what their predecessors had been attempting to do for years. York was in the doldrums. It had once been a thriving social centre, but now the aristocracy had deserted it. The assemblies had declined; the races had declined. Yet, out in the West Riding, towns were booming, great fortunes were being made out of the industries that had taken root in places like Bradford, Halifax and Leeds. York's businessmen cast envious eyes at those fortunes and asked themselves why their city was not becoming an industrial centre. Because of the high price of coal, they decided. If only the price of coal could be reduced, York would become an industrial centre and the glories of an earlier age repeated. "York is the second City in point of rank in the Kingdom, and has always been styled the capital of the North," a guide published in 1814 said, "although now left behind in wealth and population by many of the newer trading towns." "Scarcely a vessel is left to tell of the thousands that once here sought refuge from the blasts of the storm, and a mart for their commerce," said another a few years later.

The Ouse was York's main artery of trade before the appearance of the railways, and all the attempts to improve the navigation of the river had the reducing of the price of coal as a prime objective. But never enough was done, and what was spent on the river was often spent unwisely. A last burst of energy by the Ouse Navigation Trustees took place in the early 1830s when they purchased a steam dredger and set to work removing some of the shoals that made navigation difficult. Samuel Tuke, Backhouse and Rowntree created a "Mutual Marine Insurance Company" in 1834, and in February of the following year the prospectus of what came to be known as the "York and London Steam Packet Company" appeared in the press. In March 1835 the company announced that direct steam communication between York and London had started. A "York, Boroughbridge and Ripon Steam Packet Company" also commenced operations about the same time. But this last surge of activity by the Ouse Trustees and the York businessmen who banked on the Navigation being improved came too late. By 1835 the railway was well under way. At the meeting at *Tomlinson's*, James Meek made all the points about the dearness of coal having a deleterious effect on the city's development.

> "great advantage attendant on this project", he said, "would be, the reduction in the price of that necessary article of consumption, coal, and he had no doubt that York would one day become a manufacturing town, as there

> could be little obstacle when coal could be delivered here at the same expense as at Leeds. . . ."

The projected company, it was expected, would make its profits in the early days more or less entirely on coal: ". . . nett profits on passengers and every description of merchandise, &c., except coals, is about equal [only] to the expense of conveyance . . ."

Meek and his associates, then, were doing exactly what they, or their predecessors, had been trying to do for years. The alacrity with which they took to railway building was the almost inevitable reaction of the businessmen of a depressed city seeing the new means of transport as a way out of their difficulties. If the aims they had in mind then had been achieved, York would have become a factory town like Halifax or Dewsbury. When the railways did arrive, the price of coal *was* reduced, and, of course, the city remained unindustrialised. The reasons are too obvious to dwell on: the beliefs held by Tuke, Meek and Hudson were seen to be fallacious, and later generations may well be pleased they were.

It was decided to form a company, of £120,000 if the line went to South Milford, or £250,000 if it went to Leeds direct. A provisional committee was elected on which sat many of the city's leading politicians—Meek, Hotham, Hargrove and Poppleton, Liberals; Jonathan Gray and Hudson, Conservatives. Hudson was made treasurer. In August 1836 a general meeting of the shareholders of what had become the York and North Midland Company was held to elect a board of directors which included Sir John Simpson, the reigning Lord Mayor, Meek, Backhouse, Robert Davies, the Liberal town clerk who had been retained after reform, and Richard Nicholson, Hudson's brother-in-Law. Hudson was made chairman of the board. James Richardson was made solicitor to the company.

Hudson was a driving force as chairman (one of the landowners he alienated was the Lord Howdenwho stood as a Tory candidate for York in 1820), and as chairman he received most of the credit for the railway of which so much was hoped. While the line was being built Hudson was climbing gradually to power in the Corporation. He was extraordinarily fortunate that corporation reform came exactly at the right time for him. His advance was one on all fronts —politician, benefactor, railwayman and banker. Flushed with his legacy, Hudson in 1833 had turned his attention to Joint Stock banking and promoted the York Union Bank, which opened in May of that year with Sir John Lowther (who looked after the York and North Midland's Bill in Parliament) as a major depositor. The bank was later used as a main instrument in financing Hudson's schemes.

By the beginning of February 1840 there were five trains every day taking passengers to Leeds and Selby via South Milford. The first through-train from York to London ran in July of the same year. Leaving at eight in the morning and going over the roundabout Midland route, it arrived at the capital at half past nine in the evening. The first fatality on the Y. & N.M. occurred less than a week after its opening, when a train from South Milford hit John Clark of Wigginton at Brumber Hill, near Ulleskelf. The first major dispute between the directors occurred in 1839, during Hudson's second mayoralty.

The dispute took place over the running of Sunday trains. George Hudson was in favour; Tuke, Rowntree and Meek, the noncon-formists, were against. Rowntree said that the Pickering railway did not operate on Sundays, but Hudson was quick to retaliate and point out that Rowntree's two friends were both connected with businesses that ran on the Sabbath—Tuke with a gas company and Meek with a glass works that employed boilermen on Sundays. Defeated over the question of Sunday travelling, Meek resigned. It is interesting to speculate what effect this may have had on Hudson. Meek was one of the few men who might have been a check on his excesses, at least at the take-off point of his career. Meek sold his shares in the York and North Midland, and George had something to say about that when Meek's fortunes rose again, and his own were plummeting.

The early director's meetings of the York and North Midland must have been uneasy affairs. Hudson had personalised politics and fellow directors like Simpson were singled out on the Corpora-tion for bitter attacks—and Simpson was ostentatiously omitted from all the Mansion House junketings. The removal of Meek made things easier. Easily identifiable enemies are useful to the demagogue, and Hudson identified his: James Meek, Anderson, Joseph Rown-tree, Leeman, Charles Heneage Elsley, Robinson and a few others. As the years went by, these were more and more to appear as jeremiahs—people who were jealous of the great man, people whose personal spite towards King Hudson would, if they had had their way, have stopped what was good for York. Hudson behaved in the way that the archetypal trades union leader behaves according to James Burnham. He identified himself entirely with his city and what he did he did for it—that he made a fortune in the process was incidental. "He owed all to the city of York," he said in 1845, "and if it ever should become a question between railway interests and those of the city, he knew which he should prefer." Which he would prefer should have been obvious to his hearers—the remark was made during a council debate on a projected direct London to York line.

George Hudson's career as a great railwayman is dealt with else-where. Lines were taken over one after another, with Hudson promising immediate increases in dividends. Never mind that a company had been paying three per cent—shareholders were hence-forth guaranteed ten, and this when the country was deep in a slump!

By 1844, about half-way through Hudson's career as a railway-man, John Francis described his domain, which was to get even larger:

> "His influence extended seventy-six miles over the York and North Midland; fifty-one over the Hull and Selby and Leeds and Selby; over the North Midland Counties, and another, [the Birmingham and Derby Junction] one hundred and seventy-eight miles; over the Newcastle and Darlington, and the Great North of England, one hundred and eleven miles; while over the Sheffield and Rotherham, the York and Scarborough, the North British, Whitby and Pickering, it affected nearly six-hundred more, making a total of 1,016 miles, all of which were successful in paying good dividends."

In 1843 an admiring *Gazette* told its readers, shortly after the amalgamation of the three companies that became the Midland, that "shareholders are mainly indebted to Mr. Alderman Hudson. The result of his energy and talents is that an amount exceeding, we believe, £5,000,000, which before scarcely yielded 3 per cent interest per annum, will it is confidently anticipated, now pay the share-holder a dividend of 5 per cent per annum immediately, with every prospect of a considerable increase at a very early period."

A description of Hudson appeared at the height of his fame:

> "He is about five feet eight inches in height, of a stout burly frame, with a short bull-neck, surmounted by a head not conspicuous for intellectuality. His face attracts attention, and the expression of his eye is not peculiar. At first sight one dislikes him . . . Notwithstanding the sinister leer of his eyes, the ungainly frame, and the unharmonious voice, his person,
> "Howsoever rude exteriorly,
> Is the cover of a fairer mind."
> than was first imagined."

BETWEEN 1839 and 1845 George Hudson reigned supreme in York, and an inglorious era it was, even although the city became a railway centre of importance. The Railway King was the key to tremendous wealth. Men knew of his doubtful methods of account-ing—they must have done—but while the dividends rolled in they did nothing. Gradually, during those years the Liberal party almost disappeared from the city council, and men voted as they were told. The tradesmen wanted railway business, and became Hudsonians. Railway workers, when they had the vote, did as they were told (the railway workshops were opened in 1842 but did not employ large numbers for many years to come). Businessmen and profess-ional men like G.T. Andrews, who built many of Hudson's railway stations, bowed down before the great man and did his bidding. Henry Bellerby, the owner, and J.L. Foster, first a reporter and then editor of the *Gazette*, were unquestioning propagandists for him. A few were worried about their association with Hudson, and said so in private—but only in private. Such a person was Thomas Backhouse.

Backhouse (1792-1845) was a nurseryman in York, a Quaker and, it will be remembered, a signatory to the 1835 election petition criticising the activities of Hudson and his Tory colleagues. Backhouse's gardens had been on the site of York's first railway station, inside the city walls on property owned by Lady Hewley's Unitarian Charity. (Compensation paid to the Backhouses amounted to £5,700) He was a founder of a York bank and a director of the Northumberland and Durham District Bank. Backhouse had been a member of the committee that had organised the pioneer Stockton and Darlington Railway, and was an original director of the Newcastle and Berwick Company. As has already been mentioned, he also became a member of the board of the Y. and N.M. Thomas was in partnership with his more famous brother, James, who left the country for a decade between 1831 and 1841. On his return James recorded that

"My brother Thomas Backhouse had so cared for my affairs during my absence, that in a pecuniary point of view, I found them rather improved than otherwise."

Backhouse's politics were Liberal and he was returned as a Liberal councillor for Castlegate at a bye-election in 1835 (caused by the vacancies created by the first aldermanic elections). Backhouse never spoke out against Hudson's excesses either as a railwayman or politician, despite his belief in "purity of election" concepts and his support for temperance (James was also noted temperance worker and a campaigner against Church rates). Backhouse never spoke out, yet it is clear that he was worried by the methods of the Railway King. Towards the end of his life, his daughter Mary recorded that her father, deeply troubled by what he saw going on around him, sought opportunities for retirement, and "most earnestly prayed for preservation from the evils which surrounded him."

The sway that Hudson exercised over the city can be seen by simply looking at the results of the annual municipal elections. Gradually the Liberals lost heart completely. In November 1841 there was not a contest in any ward in the city (the Conservatives ostentatiously refraining from challenging the few Liberal councillors and candidates seeking election). In 1842 the Liberals made no challenge at all in the four strong Tory wards of Guildhall, Bootham, Monk and Walmgate. In 1845 James Chadwick, Jethro Heseltine and John Meek, all dyed-in-the-wool Hudsonians, went unchallenged. In 1846 again there was no contest anywhere in the city. By this time Hudson had altered his tack. Early on it had paid him to heighten feelings and present his opponents as enemies of Yo k. Later he calmed things down, when men had been won over, telling them, Baldwin-like, not to rock the boat. They hardly needed telling that.

In the mid-forties Hudson seemed to be unassailable and the voices of Meek, Leeman, Rowntree, Tuke and the *Yorkshireman* were muted. There were always a few people in the city independent of the great man, who could have kept up a running a criticism of him and his methods, and it is not to the credit of the people like Rowntree and Tuke that they did not do so. Perhaps they were biding their time, waiting for the King's inevitable mistakes. But it was a person much more humble than any of these who eventually led the attack on him.

The opposition in the council, with very few exceptions, was an opposition in name only. In 1845, the relative strength of the parties was Conservatives 34, Liberals 14, but many of those 14 were Liberals who supported Hudson unquestioningly. During the early 1840s one after another had jumped on to the Hudson bandwaggon, enabling the Railway King to talk of all-party support for himself. Robert Davies, the long-serving clerk to the council, forgot his Liberalism when the Tories took over. As will be seen later, in an important crucial debate in 1845, only three Liberals stood up to Hudson. Henry Cobb became a Hudson man, and so did Backhouse and Robert Henry Anderson. The latter prostrated himself at the feet of the man who had attacked him and his religion as bitterly as he had attacked anyone. Anderson had been Hudson's *bête noir* for years, and his muling, whining, creeping attitude to the the man who so kicked him makes pathetic reading. But Anderson always miscalculated. He declared himself too late to benefit; George was almost over the top when Robert Henry put on his livery.

The Hudson methods might be looked at again. The personal attacks were mentioned in a debate on the council in which the Liberals opposed a vote of thanks to Hudson at the end of his second mayoralty. Sir John Simpson told the council that he thought Hudson had been re-elected a second time "by a viscious perversion of the law" and mentioned again that he was never invited to parties at the Mansion House (now "a blue committee room" according to the *Yorkshireman*). Charles James Hanson had been similarly ignored, and Alderman Wilson (Liberal) said that he had suffered continually throughout the year from Hudson's biting tongue. "Whether in public or private, at committee meetings, in the streets, or at private dinner parties, Mr. Hudson had made a determined point of insulting him; wherever they had dined, he had always been the object of Mr. Hudson's taunts and insulting language." Next to Anderson, however, Hudson hated Charles Heneage Elsley most of all.

Elsley was Recorder of York and a co-director, with Hudson, of the York Union Gas-Light Company; he was also a director of railway companies that were outside Hudson's control. Unlike the pliable Robert Davies, Elsley had refused to become a Hudson man. In February 1840 a dinner, held at the Guildhall to celebrate the marriage of Queen Victoria, was ruined by Hudson's show of "purse proud vulgarity" that shocked even his admirers. Elsley had tendered apologies for the non-appearance of Lord Wenlock, the Liberal Lord Lieutenant of Yorkshire, and later had the misfortune to have to propose the toast of "Her Majesty's [Whig] Ministers." Hudson refused to drink the latter and launched a furious attack on the Recorder. Elsley's "aristocratical" connections were dragged up—he was a relative of the Dundas family—and the assembly witnessed a scene which the *Courant* said beggared description—"all we can say is, that we rarely, if ever, saw such a scene before the hustings during a contested election." The same issue of the newspaper that reported the dreadful Guildhall scene recorded an attempt by Henry Bellerby (councillor for Guildhall from 1836) on the council to cut the Recorder's salary!

Hudson's own colleagues in the Conservative party were dragooned as unmercifully as his workmen. John Wolstenholme got a severe drubbing for not initially supporting Hudson's nominee for the post of schoolmaster of St. Crux's, and was ordered how to vote. Reminding the council of a speech Hudson had made at Kirbymoorside, in which he boasted that he had "Conservatised the whole city" of York, George Leeman, mocking people like Wolstenholme, urged them to "Fall down then, ye conservatives, fall down upon the golden calf which you have set up! You are an ungrateful set of men if you don't." Peter Rymer, an unswerving Hudsonian, said that Leeman had "so scandalized the Lord Mayor, that if he had been one of the decendants of Cain he could not have given him a worse character." The St. Crux school incident filled many columns of newsprint. But Hudson had not only interfered in the appointment of a schoolmaster, he had also "fixed" the appointment of a keeper at the Festival Concert Room, and secured the post for a good (Conservative) party man. This was in 1839. He had also that year fixed the municipal revision.

Hudson, as Lord Mayor, presided at the revision of October 1839. The ward associations of the newly created York Liberal Association had been active preparing for the revision and had worked well. 118 objections were to be made on behalf of the Liberals, but the notices of objection handed in read, "I object to the name of . . . being retained on the Burgess List." Hudson maintained they should have read "Citizens' List" and disallowed the objections in all but one ward (Micklegate). As the elections were to be fought within a month of the revision there was no time for legal proceedings. Out of the 118, only 8 objections were sustained. At the subsequent elections, William Blanshard, a barrister, was returned as a new Tory recruit. He told the council that he was sure Hudson's act was not a partisan one: ". . . he believed in his heart that the Lord Mayor had acted to the best of his judgement, and that he was incapable of acting from corrupt and dishonest motives." Blanshard's words would have stuck in his throat had he had the benefit of foresight. Alderman Swann, speaking at the same time, struck a more realistic note (Swann was a banker). "Mr. Hudson was a strong party man; no man had done more for the party which he support[ed] than the late Lord Mayor." At the election fought on the list Hudson had doctored, the Tories secured eight out of the 12 seats contested

Two years after this, with the Railway King more securely in power than ever before, a general election took place. The Liberal Government had run out of steam, was unpopular and the party was divided between hostile Whig and radical factions. It is quite certain that many of the Conservatives in York wanted Hudson to run with Lowther. There is no doubt that Hudson himself wanted to do so, to crown a meteoric and sensational career. With the tide running for the Tories (and with his bottomless purse) it is certain he would have got in. But it was not to be.

The York Conservatives had prior obligations to David Francis Atcherley, who had stood in 1837. Atcherley was a Sergeant-at-Law who had been called up to run with Lowther in a most extraordinary election. None of the higher eschelons of the Conservative party had appeared at the meetings that decided to requisition him; no-one like Cattle, Wolstenholme or Hudson had worked on his committees. Later it transpired that Hudson had pulled the wool over the Liberal leaders' eyes. Elsley said that "the Magnate of Monkgate" had assured him that there would be no contest, and that if Atcherley went to a poll, Lowther would retire. If two Tories were started, Hudson and his colleagues would split with Dundas. He (Hudson) had nothing to do with the calling up of Atcherley. The Liberals believed him. But Atcherley *did* go to a poll, and Hudson and the others, despite their promises, voted for both Tories!

The election of 1837 is shrouded in mystery, as is Hudson's behaviour at that time. Afterwards, and this is a strange occurrence, Atcherley, the Tory, contemplated petitioning against the successful Liberal on the grounds of corruption. An enquiry might well have shown Dundas bribing, but it would have condemned Lowther too, and Lowther had had a big enough scare in 1835. Atcherley eventually dropped the idea of petitioning. Another election could not be far away. Support in York, and an assured candidacy, seems to have been the price he was paid.

The great issue of the election of 1841 was free trade. The York Liberals had refused to commit themselves when the Melbourne Government was in power, but now they came out as advocates for repeal of the corn laws. Their candidate was Henry Redhead Yorke, and people like George Leeman and Elsley showed that the pleadings of the Anti-Corn Law League had had their effect. York had received the attentions of prominent League lecturers like J.S. Buckingham regularly since 1839, and petitions had gone from the city demanding repeal.

The Liberal stand infuriated the organised working-class movement. To the Chartists the Anti-Corn Law League was an organisation got up by Whig manufacturers who cried "cheap bread" when they really meant "cheap labour," and at the election of 1841 they supported, very often, Tory candidates. They did so in York. The Chartist movement in Hudson's city was not very large—it could hardly be so where his baneful influence prevailed and where there was no large industry—but the Chartists there took the same line as they did elsewhere. James Leach of Manchester, a well-known leader, was brought into the constituency to reply to the arguments of the free traders. On polling day, the *Courant* said

'These dupes of unprincipled leaders ... waited until the afternoon to see how the poll proceeded, and then, when circumstances showed that they might manifest their 'spite', they went as a body and voted for the Tory candidate."

So Hudson's party would receive some unexpected, unsolicited and unpaid for votes, but overall the methods of influencing the electorate were as usual—intimidation, personating and bribing. Corporation tenants were told what to do: "... as the corporation was blue ... not to vote against the blues." Richard Hornby, Tory councillor for Monk, demanded that Matthew Summerwell, his barber, should vote conservative, but Summerwell refused. He eventually received a letter from Hornby saying that "Mr. Hornby desires Mr. Summerwell will *send* his bill in for shaving, and never enter Mr. Hornby's door any more."

The Liberals must also have bribed on a grand scale to have done as well as they did. It is strange to read the following comments from George Hudson, who knew about these things: "The Conservatives had been beat [they wanted both seats], but they were not beat with fair weapons—their opponents resorted to corruption and bribery of the most infamous kind—bribery stalked in our streets." (A recent work on York makes the erroneous statement that Hudson during his reign of power "ensured that only Tory" MPs represented York, but even Hudson was never able to achieve this degree of success).

Yorke, Atcherley and Lowther stood, the Liberals not daring to run a second candidate in the prevailing political climate. Hudson proposed Lowther at the hustings, and when it was all over York was still represented by a member from each party. Only 169 votes separated Lowther at the top of the poll from Atcherley at the bottom.

Denied York, Hudson eventually entered Parliament as member for Sunderland. Earl Grey passed away in July 1845 and his son, Lord Howick, member for Sunderland, succeeded him. R.S. Lambert says that Hudson had his eye on Whitby at the time, but when the Sunderland opportunity arose it seems that he had high hopes, once more, of York being his. Rumours were flying that Lowther was to be awarded a peerage for his unwavering support of Sir Robert Peel and the reversion would certainly have been Hudson's.

> "We have never had occasion to call in question the consistency of Sir JOHN LOWTHER, so far as his votes are concerned," wrote the *Yorkshireman*. "He is one of those gentlemen, who, in season and out of season, studiously awaits divisions, and follows Sir ROBERT PEEL with an almost affectionate attention. Let the Right Hon. Baronet wander into the realms of free trade, radical reform, or leap, on the other hand into ultra-toryism, there is Sir JOHN LOWTHER following him with a chivalrous devotion worthy of—let us see! —worthy of what? *Of a Peerage!*"

Hudson stood at Sunderland as a dyed-in-the-wool protectionist and the contest turned into a fight between protection and free trade. "I consider the proposition of Free Trade a most wild and visionary thing," Hudson said, "I consider it neither more nor less than an attempt to throw the land out of cultivation." The Anti-Corn Law League moved in Colonel Perronet Thompson, one of their really big guns. The contest was said to have cost the Railway King £10,000. Hundreds of helpers flooded into Sunderland in trains from York, and J.H. Lowther aided him. Richard Cobden wrote during the election of the overwhelming influence that Colonel Thompson had to contend with:

> "A more formidable opponent he could not have had ... than this Railway King—He [went] into the constituency with an *intangible* bribe for every class—The Capitalist would hope for premiums—The smaller fry would look for situations for their sons in the vast railway undertakings over which he rules absolutely, and the rope, iron, coal, and timber merchants all bid for his patronage—His *undetectable* powers of corruption ... are greater than the prime minister's. I would rather face any man than Hudson in a contest."

Hudson's comments on the election to his admiring followers in York referred to Cobden as "the O'Connell of England." He fought, he said,

> "an enemy exceedingly crafty, and not very scrupulous ... whose object has not been the truth but to deceive the people—men who have no regard for private character, nor as to the means by which they might carry out the object they had in view."

Hudson told the Sunderland electors after his return why he went to them and sought their votes: ". . . it is BECAUSE I have made a fortune and am independent that I come here to ask for your suffrages to send me to Parliament—*that there I may crown all.*" His return to York was sensational. It underlined his dominance there and the way most of his opponents had been won over. The chastened Sir John Simpson had now come to heel and was there to greet him and congratulate him. By now William Hargrove had joined the throng, even though remaining nominally a Liberal, and the *Courant* and the *Herald* were as fawning in their attitude to Hudson as was the *Gazette*.

But the days were shortening for Hudson and it is possible to contend that his return to Parliament was one of his first great mistakes. In the mid-forties, while the "railway mania" was at its height, Hudson went unchallenged. Political issues were subdued and men would not have listened to criticism of their idol. He pontificated on railway matters, and in York critics would have been accused of rocking the boat. In Parliament, however, he would be expected to pass judgement on wider issues, and the *Yorkshireman*, which had not had a good crack at him for years, looked forward to his giving them their opportunity. His experience there might have a salutary effect it said:

> "Out of Parliament he (is) a great man ... wielding immense influence. In Parliament he will be nobody and destitute of all influence. He will discover this himself bye and bye. It will be quite a different thing to address a meeting of railway speculators panting for ten per cent, and the congregated intellect, learning and gentlemanly accomplishments such as the British Parliament contains. Men find their level in the House of Commons, and Mr. HUDSON will find his. Perhaps, too, it may do him good."

The *Yorkshireman* was not disappointed. Hudson had been returned as an arch protectionist, and in the Commons he took it upon himself to act as the spokesman for the agriculturalists. He entered Parliament when the brilliant Anti-Corn Law League campaign for free trade was reaching its climax. Peel had decided to remove the corn laws at the end of 1845. On 5 December he resigned, but was back in power within 15 days to carry repeal and brave the wrath of people like the Railway King. In February Peel laid before the House a "searching, crushing exposure of the fallacies so glibly enunciated by the confederated Protectionists, "the *Yorkshireman* said, whereupon Hudson,a "sort of Lilliputian in the land of Gulliver's adventures "inflicted "upon the House two ponderous columns of the *Morning Post*—those columns comprising an aggregate of the veriest rubbish which ever mortal muttered."

Hudson cut a sorry figure in Parliament. The *Yorkshireman* made fun of his diction and his bad grammar, and challenged his facts. In one speech he had said that a friend of his, a paper-stainer in York, had had to lay workmen off because of the threat of free trade. His friend was easily identified as Henry Cobb, an erstwhile Liberal who had been won over, and the *Yorkshireman* had no difficulty at all in proving that he had not sacked anyone! Similarly, it was able to show that Hudson had pulled the wool over the Commons' eyes about a deal of his involving imported corn. It also made no bones about George's over-indulgence on occasion—a shrewd move in York, where there was a very strong and influential temperance movement. It was a temperance man who eventually took on Hudson and proved his greatest enemy—in York at any rate.

The Railway King was being turned into a figure of fun by Leeman and his associates on the *Yorkshireman;* his return to Parliament had given them the chance they had been waiting for for years. Further opportunities came their way when Hudson, bloated with success, began to make a series of grave mistakes. 1845 was his very greatest year, but it was also the first year in which real murmurings about his methods, his motives and his allegiances began to be heard. A year which his admirers should find difficult to explain away.

AT a quarterly meeting of the York Corporation in February 1845 the question of the proposed London to York railway was raised. This was the brainchild of Edmund Beckitt Denison, MP, which first saw the light of day in 1844. Planned to run through St. Neots and Peterborough to York, it was an obvious and serious threat to Hudson's lines. "The long circuitous route between London and York via Rugby, Derby and Normanton, would be hard put to retain the through traffic to the north, if ever the line through Peterborough ... were made." The proposed new line would link up, in Hudson's own city, with one of its other railways, the Great North of England. Hudson promptly bought up the line at an incredibly inflated price, as a strategic move. He paid "such princely terms" for the Great North of England, "which had been doing poorly," Hamilton Ellis wrote, "that their £100 shares rose within the space of a few months from par to £144 premium." Hudson's shady dealing in Great North of England shares was a major cause of his eventual downfall and disgrace.

Henry Cobb brought the London and York to the notice of councillors. He declared that he was not a shareholder in the threatened York and North Midland, but made it quite clear that he was the spokesman of many who were. Cobb's duty was to persuade the city corporation to petition against the new railway. "He thought," he said, "the city of York was very much indebted to the projectors of the present [York and North Midland] line, and that they ought to have some regard for those," like his leader, "who had a stake in it ... He understood that there was no less than a quarter of a million held by inhabitants of this city and neighbourhood in the present line." Hudson had a monopoly and his lackeys wanted him to keep it. Hudson also acted as a monopolist, and kept prices high, something for which he was put on the block by the *Times*--a confrontation between "the railway Potentate and the literary Potentate of Printing House Square" that the *Yorkshireman* recounted with great gusto. Simpson, the nominal leader of the opposition, supported Cobb, calling the London and York "an absurd and monstrous scheme," a "wild goose and filching scheme." W.S. Matterson revealed that he had once been a York and North Midland shareholder, "but had unfortunately sold out," and he lent his support. (Matterson, if only he had known it, was lucky to have sold out). 25 persons voted for the petition. The relative strength of the parties at the time was nominally 34 : 14.

Only four person's opposed the petition against the new scheme, one Tory and three Liberals. The Tory was Alderman Swann, a shareholder (£5,000) in the London and York. Henry Smales was one of the Liberals and James Meek was another—the same James Meek who had been a prime mover in the York and North Midland and who had resigned over the question of Sunday travel. Having satisfied himself on the projected London and York's attitude to Sunday trains, he and his son had taken £12,000 of shares in it. George Leeman, another shareholder (£2,500), was the fourth member of the tiny "opposition." Hudson's reply to them was rude, blustering, and to his doting followers utterly convincing. "Voluble, he is," a contemporary biography of him said, "but it is the loquacity of a country ploughboy excited by potations, . . . no one thinks of questioning the Railway Monarch." But these four had!

Leeman said York would gain enormously from the new line and a London and York railway station would have to be built in the city at an expenditure of £50,000. What was this compared with the benefits bestowed through the York and North Midland, Hudson demanded. The York and North Midland was directed by men like himself, he said, "men whose feelings and interests were blended with those of the citizens of York." Swann and his fellow subscribers to the new railway were enemies of York's best interests:

"Where were these gentlemen of the London and York line when the York and Norh Midland was formed?" asked Hudson, "where was Mr. Swann when the shares were at a discount, and when many of the projectors of the line stood trembling in their shoes? Where was Mr. Swann when the Midland was at a discount? Not advocating railway communications for the public. No, but as soon as they saw the railway would assume a profitable appearance, they aroused from their slumbers and said, 'We will make a railway too, and if we can't get such a one as will be profitable, we will make such a one as will destroy that already in existence."

Meek, the Railway King said, had sold his shares in the York and North Midland at a profit, then set up in opposition to it. "I could have retired and followed your example," Hudson claimed, "but

I should have been a monument of eternal disgrace to the city of York had I done so." He had been "charged with wishing to sacrifice the interests of his fellow citizens for the promotion of his own," Hudson said, certain that the Mattersons, the Rymers and the Richardsons would be shocked at the suggestion

> "and he appealed to the council whether he had ever committed any act that would justify that aspersion: he could only say that if he had he should have been ashamed of himself as long as he lived ... He owed all to the city of York, and if it ever should become a question between railway interests and those of the city, he knew which he should prefer."

Prophetic words.

Hudson had used his control of the Corporation and made it petition against what surely were York's long-term interests. And he was thanked for doing so, and rewarded by being nominated as Lord Mayor for a third time! When the new council met after the 1846 elections, his name was suggested by Alderman Gray. Hudson had ruled before, Gray said, in stormy times, but recently the council had "shut out of [its chamber] ... those subjects which lead to discussions of a painful nature." William Stephenson Clark overlooked the efforts of people like Meek and gave Hudson all the credit for York's revival over the decade or so that had passed. His "great feature," Clark said, had "been that noble display of railway powers which he [had] introduced and concentrated within the walls of York, and but for which [York] would now have been tantamount to a deserted village, whereas it might now justly be termed the Queen of Railway towns." This is precisely the kind of statement made by modern-day admirers of the Railway King. But the York and North Midland, as has been shown, was not Hudson's brainchild. The city at the time had two other lines (two others were under construction: one was Hudson's; the other—the York to Market Weighton—was originally planned by Captain Laws, one of Hudson's competitors). That to Scarborough and Whitby was one of his "cherished projects," but the Great North of England owed its creation not to Hudson but to Joseph Pease and a group of northern Quakers—who saw the merits of York as a railway centre. As if to emphasise the dominance of the railways over the city, George choose G.T. Andrews, the railway architect, as his Sheriff.

The Corporation had done his bidding over the petition against the London and York Railway. At the very meeting at which he was elected as Lord Mayor again, Hudson, without prior notice of any kind, introduced another scheme for which he expected unquestioning support. This was a proposal to bridge the river Ouse at Lendal ferry. And this was mistake number three. Getting into Parliament had given his enemies the chance to poke fun at him. Making the council petition against a competitor had re-activated the small group of radicals outside his control. Now his behaviour was to give them even greater opportunities to hit out at him.

THE river Ouse was crossed by only one bridge in the 1840s. At Lendal there was a ferry, and there had periodically been proposals put forward to bridge the river there before Hudson re-introduced the topic in late 1846. In September 1838 Robert Cattle, the great coach proprietor, created the New Bridge Company with a capital of £3,500 which intended to cross the Ouse at Lendal with a suspension bridge for pedestrians. With a railway station being built inside the walls near to Lendal, some means of crossing the river was obviously necessary, but something more substantial tham a footbridge was needed. The Corporation decided that it should be erected by the authority and not a private company, and Cattle's company was dissolved. In 1840 the two railway companies (the York and North Midland and the Great North of England), it was discovered, intended to apply to Parliament for the requisite powers to bridge the river, but a factious opposition led by George Leeman representing people with interests in Micklegate defeated it, and nothing more was heard for six years.

Hudson sprang the new proposal for a Lendal bridge on the doting councillors who had just re-elected him. It was a necessary, long-overdue improvement to the city, he said. Not only would it make access to the railway station simpler, it would open up the approach to the Minster. The approach to the bridge from the Minster side should be widened and improved by means of a public subscription, which he would head with a donation of £500. The Yorkshire Insurance Company would lend £4,000 at four per cent, and property values in the area would rise even more than they had already. The railway company, of course, would contribute. The Lord Mayor proposed that the council should apply for an Act to enable the work to go ahead.

Robert Henry Anderson (defeated in 1844 but returned a year later when Thomas Backhouse died) wanted to know how much the railway company would actually guarantee—the cost of obtaining the Bill alone, he thought, would be £1,000. "Mr. Ald. HUDSON . . . observed that if the council would leave the matter in his hands," the *Gazette* recorded, "he would take care that the city should not suffer. He was not prepared to say what the extent would be, nor what the railway company would subscribe." The great man had spoken; his word was his bond—and that was good enough for most of the council. "Mr. Ald. Hudson's explanation was entirely satisfactory to his mind," Anderson said, "and the reliance which he had upon Mr. Ald. Hudson's assurance was very great." W.S. Clark said that "after what his excellent friend (Ald. Hudson) had said, and after what he had done for the good of the city, he thought there was no-one who could offer any opposition in earnest." Clark was wrong. R.S. Lambert says that Hudson's resolution was passed unanimously, but it was not. Three persons voted against it, and James Meek said he would have done so, too, had he been there.

The three were Charles Robinson whom Hudson had had thrown off the council (he had got back in 1844); Smales, one of those who had opposed the petition against the London and York; and George Leeman.

Leeman slammed into Hudson, accusing him of falsifying figures and estimates, and behaving dictatorially. The bridge would cost between £20,000 and £30,000 he said, far more than Hudson had hinted at. The bridge was for the convenience of the railway company, not the city, and Leeman reminded his hearers that in 1840 and 1841 the two companies had been prepared to foot the whole bill. He complained of the cavalier fashion in which the latest proposal had been introduced at the last possible moment. The bit between his teeth, Leeman said it had been discussed by the city's Finance Committee less than a month before and he furiously resented the fact that "a measure so greatly affecting the pecuniary interests of the city, should be brought forward in the council chamber, for the first time, on the very last day before that on which they ought to give notice of their application to Parliament. The Town Clerk [Robert Davies] knew very well that unless his notices were posted that night they would be too late." Hudson had been treating the council this way for years. But this time he had gone too far. His behaviour over the petition and his behaviour in Parliament had rallied up an opposition. This latest brick was a Godsend to them.

The furore over the Lendal bridge continued outside the council chamber. Leeman created a committee to watch over any proposals that might be produced and in November the Liberals revealed what they claimed were Hudson's real motives for wanting the bridge—in part admitted by him already anyway. The opposition had been called the agents of the "London and Great Northern Railway Company" and some were shareholders in it, it was well known. The royal assent to their Bill to take another line into Hudson's city had been given in June 1846. Hudson's lobbying and petitioning had only had the effect of delaying the Act, and now, chastened, he was out to steal a march on his rivals. The London and York's station would be sited in Trinity Gardens, Micklegate, and by building the new bridge Hudson's station would have a superior approach. It was as simple as that. "Thus, then, the citizens know the whole secret. They are to be taxed because Mr. Hudson doesn't like the London and York scheme," said the *Yorkshireman.* "Very well," it went on,

> "Mr. Hudson is accustomed to speak contemptuously of the power of the press. We shall see, however, if we cannot strangle this disgraceful job in the bud. The hon. member has his corporation toadies, but the citizens are not compelled to wear his badge."

Many were, but Hudson had not been attacked like this for years— ". . . the depth of . . . flunkeyism, towards Mr. Hudson, begins to assume a rather alarming aspect," the *Yorkshireman* contended

"In railway matters, wherein the hon. member, invariably is putting into his own and familiar friends pockets, dictation, perhaps, may be endured, but we think it will reflect the utmost discredit upon the city if it permits itself passively to be taxed for the errection of an edifice for the convenience of the York and North Midland Railway Company . . . It is quite clear that there is nothing to be expected from the Town Council. The majority of members of that body are so devoted to his Railway Majesty that, had he suggested a silver bridge across Lendal Ferry, they would have bent their necks and cried 'aye' to the proposition."

In December—the speed with which all this was done was incredible—a plan for the new bridge was made public. But who was to foot the bill? Leeman and the *Yorkshireman* demanded that the York and North Midland pay—it was "fat and flourishing," paying the ten per cent maximum to which it was restricted. It had been prepared to do so (the Great North of England had been bought up now, of course) in 1840, and should do so now: ". . . is it that he [Hudson] is sufficiently vain-glorious as to display the amount of dirt through which his followers are willing to wade at his bidding?" On this occasion he bowed before the storm.

A council meeting was held in December 1846 at which it was announced that the outcry of Leeman and his friends had had an effect. The railway company agreed to pay for the bridge and approaches to it on the south-west side of the river. Leeman accepted the offer, as did Smales, Robinson and James Meek. (Only one person was against doing so). Hudson had "received a severe lesson," said the *Yorkshireman*, "He has discovered that he is not quite so great a man as he suspected himself." Earlier it had talked of the "liveried-toadies" of the corporation. "We have been told that we wear the livery of your lordship," Robert Henry Anderson told Hudson, "and that there are only two or three independent persons on the council who do not wear that livery. . . . I do not think there is anything disgraceful in wearing that livery." That must be the most explicit statement of sycophancy from the whole Hudson era. Robert Henry, who had for years been the object of some of the Railway King's bitterest harangues, had gone over.

Hudson's strategic withdrawal was out of character but effective. His next mistakes were irredeemable. Those of 1845 and 1846 were glossed over by his grateful toadies, and his critics were execrated by Bellerby and the *Gazette*, and the Hargrove newspapers (embarrassed by the Lendal bridge affair, Hargrove had simply not reported it). What did it matter if the council was in the pocket of the Railway King, if he still had the Midas touch? It seemed that Hudson might be learning tact—but in 1847 he showed that he had learned nothing from his experiences of '45 and '46. From that time what was needed in York was the velvet glove technique. In 1847, however, Hudson used the mailed fist with a vengeance. So far he had activated a

small group of Liberals who thought (and invested) differently from
the way he did. Now he was to alienate in turn members of his own
party, then the populace at large, until a massive attack was launched
against him and his position. And he did this when the first murmurings about his railway financing began to be national news.

IN February 1847 the *Yorkshireman* (alone of York's newspapers)
reported the suspicious "juggling in railway finance" that surrounded the purchase of the Newcastle and Berwick Railway by the
York and Newcastle line. "We beg to direct attention to a special
report," the editorial said,

> "of an extraordinary railway meeting held in Manchester on Wednesday last. It
> is worth perusal from the startling facts it discloses in railway management.
> Among other strange circumstances which came out at the meeting, was, that
> Mr. George Hudson had had allotted to him, at his own request, 1,000 shares;
> that he had signed the deed for that amount; but that he had never paid a
> farthing of deposit-another gentleman performing that obligation, and he re-
> taining the shares. Ha! ye small fry of railway stags rejoice, and clap your
> hands with joy. The Railway King is at your head. Yes, in verity, he is the
> 'royal railway stag!'—'To what base uses must we come at last, Horatio?'
> But more of this anon."

Hudson never learned to ignore criticism even when that was the
wisest course of action. He punished his critics and withdrew railway
advertisements from the *Newcastle Advertiser*, the *Gateshead Obser-
ver*, and, of course, the *Yorkshireman*. "The Royal Dogberry and
the Press" was the latter's heading of its account of the latest act
of this "headstrong and arrogant man." The York Union Bank
withdrew its advertisements in February and this spiteful behaviour
was fuel for Leeman and his colleagues who produced columns of
print as they laid into "His Steam Majesty" week after week. As
early as January 1847 they announced that they were making plans
to oust York's favourite son, who was just beginning to show the
country at large that he had feet of clay, from his dominant position
in the city. "The Council Chamber," the *Yorkshireman* declared,
"must be purged of its obsequious members" at the November
elections

> "or else there is no knowing but Mr. Hudson may some day take it into his head
> to seize the Minster, and convert it into a station for the York and North
> Midland Company. Of one thing we are quite sure that did he propose so
> extravagant a seizure, there are a few, if any, of his municipal vassals who
> would cry 'nay'!"

In June the York newspapers carried an announcement from J.H.
Lowther saying that he would not stand as a candidate at any future
election. He was retiring, he said, because he could not find it in
himself to oppose the government of the day. After Sir Robert Peel

had carried the repeal of the corn laws, the protectionists had turned
on him and ousted him from office. At the time Lowther wrote, a
Liberal government under Lord John Russell was in existence, kept
in office by the support of those Conservatives who had followed
Peel into the wilderness. Among those was John Henry Lowther. He
hinted darkly that he had been dictated to about how to vote.

Alongside Lowthers' announcement was another from John
George Smyth of Heath Hall, Wakefield, saying that he intended to
present himself at York in the conservative interest whenever a
general election was called. Who was this Smyth, the Liberals
asked. Born in 1815, he had been educated at Eton and Trinity
College, Cambridge, and was the son of a member for that University
and the grandson of a member for Pontefract. But there was more.
"We may add," said the *Yorkshireman*,

> "that he his *the* Mr. Smyth who has put forward, nominally, as the opposer
> of the London and York, and Wakefield, Pontefract, and Goole lines-Mr.
> Hudson paying his expenses! We wonder if a like compact has been entered
> into with respect to the representation of this city? Alas! poor spiritless
> Tories!—how high-minded it is thus to suffer yourselves to be bought and
> sold-to be kicked and cuffed just as suits the fancy of your slave-driving
> leader."

Immediately after these announcements appeared, rumours began
that Lowther was being thrown over by Hudson because they were
now in opposite political camps—Lowther a Peelite; Hudson a
protectionist, a follower of Lord George Bentinck and the group of
Conservatives which eventually coalesced around Disraeli. The
choice of Smyth seemed to leave no doubt in the minds of the
sceptical. But to many, despite the fact that suspicions of "railway
juggling" attached themselves to him, Hudson could still do no
wrong. All would be well when he explained what had happened.

With the *Yorkshireman* snarling angrily at his heels, Hudson
attended a conservative election committee meeting. Only a reporter
from the *Gazette* was allowed to be present, and Hudson explained
why Lowther had resigned. (Why Lowther was not allowed to do so
himself was presumably because there was no question of the
party as a whole being sympathetic to a Peelite). Hudson said that
he had never discussed the question of corn law repeal with Lowther
and that the latter was resigning because of ill health. (The first
Lowther announcement had said nothing about ill health). The only
time the Raiway King and York's senior M.P. had discussed important political issues, Hudson said, was when that thorny question
of early Victorian politics came up—the grant to the Roman Catholic College of Maynooth. Hudson's critics were quick to point out
that Lowther had voted "for" when the question first appeared,
and "against" on the second occasion—against, it was assumed,
when George cracked his whip.

As over the Lendal bridge affair, Hudson's followers were completely satisfied with his explanation. W.S. Clark said that he, and
many more, had hoped that Hudson himself would stand for York,
and some *had* had doubts about the treatment of Lowther—until
they had heard the truth from their leader! What they wanted for
York was a Tory who would not follow Peel, on whom no abuse
was good enough these days. The *Yorkshireman* was not as convinced as Clark. "It was Mr. Hudson who forced the Hon. gentleman
to do violence to his conscience, and place himself in a most humiliating condition," it said. Hargrove and the *Herald*, however, were
as satisfied as were the Clarks and the Husbands. "We have great
pleasure in stating that all those reports [of undue influence] were
without foundation," its readers were told.

Smyth presented himself as an ultra Tory, and his views, as stated
by the *Gazette*, must have stretched even Robert Henry Anderson's
allegiance to his new mentor, the man behind Smyth. At the election
committee already referred to, George Hudson made a "No Popery"
speech (it appeared at that time that this was to be, yet again, a main
plank of Tory electioneering, and it will be recalled that Lowther
had differed with Hudson over the catholic question—until dragged
into line). Smyth followed in a similar vein. "On the great question
of Protestantism Mr. SMYTH was clear and explicit. . . . He will
oppose all concessions to Popery."

The Conservatives were split, and their prospects at the general
election which Russell prompted in July, could not have looked good
—and this may be why they raised the old, and very useful bogey,
of No Popery. The Railway King and his colleagues, however, let
it be known that they did not want a contest, and that they would
be satisfied with shared representation. During the Hudson years the
Liberals had become depleted as more and more had jumped on to the
railway bandwagon, their electoral organisation (which had always
been poor) disappeared, and the Dundas's and Fitzwilliams were
no longer available to foot the bills for expensive contests. The
Liberals too were prepared to settle for one seat and no contest.
Yorke was chosen to stand again and in the weeks before the
election no further candidates were introduced.

A quiet election was intended, but during the canvass Smyth was
given a rough time. In an attempt to win favour he included the abol-
ition of church rates (something very dear to the Quakers) among
his demands, but this was not nearly enough. Clark and Husband
were active on Smyth's behalf and they were continually interrupted
with cries of "Lowther." Anderson, Hargrove and the rest may have
been satisfied that Hudson had not thrown Lowther out, but the
populace at large were convinced that he had.

However much the older members among the Liberals may have
gone over to the Railway King, the very fact of a general election
taking place forced them to take at least a nominal stand against

Smyth, and therefore Hudson. This is another reason why they did not want a contest. Henry Redhead Yorke was supported by William Hargrove, John Wood, the coroner, and Sir John Simpson, among others who must have felt acutely embarrassed at opposing the man they had so obviously sold out to years ago. And they had to do this, fortuitously, just at a time when Hudson was coming under heavy fire for really the first time in his career—nationally (although there was but the ground swell as yet) for his railway fiddles, and locally because of his behaviour over Lendal, the London and York railway and Lowther. The opposition of people like Simpson, nominal though it might have been, must have had a tremendous psychological impact on Hudson. It might have looked a much more serious desertion than it was. It may explain the extraordinary ham-handed, short-sighted way Hudson behaved at the hustings.

The hustings were held in St. Sampson's Square before a crowd estimated at between 6,000 and 8,000 people. Yorke was nominated by Simpson and T.W. Wilson, and then Hudson stepped forward to propose the latest addition to his entourage. There ensued scenes of indescribable confusion, and Hudson had to be protected from the crowd by the police. The great man had gone too far, for the impossible had happened, he was howled down in his own city. Hudson's treatment of him had had the incredible effect of turning the reactionary Lowther (against the reform act, against catholic emancipation) into a popular figure! "Gentlemen, I claim a hearing at your hands," said the Lord Mayor "for I know of nothing I have done to forfeit that respect which has ever been evinced towards me." But he *was* refused a hearing and James Chadwick had just enough time to assure the crowd that Smyth would "protect [their] Protestantism" before he, too, was howled down.

At this stage the proceedings should, in effect, have ended. All that was intended afterwards was a ritual-proposing, seconding, speech-making and declaration—and York's part in the general election would have been over, and Smyth and Yorke returned. But at this stage, Frederick Hopwood stood up and proposed John Henry Lowther. If York is really looking for a politician to honour it could do worse than look at Hopwood, even if his name does not scan as well as Hudson's when attached to a street name.

Frederick Hopwood had been around in York for a number of years. Originally from Pocklington, he was a paid temperance, or rather teetotall, organiser and speaker. York, like most Victorian cities, had a fantastic number of pubs and beer houses. It had areas of dreadful overcrowding, and it had nightly riots that often, in the late forties took on the appearance of race riots—"Erin versus Ebor." The Bedern was an area of regular Saturday night drunken brawls, a red-light district (the brothels, the nonconformists delightedly pointed out, were on church property,) where the Irish settled after the great famine. The Water Lanes, another red-light area, and Walmgate, were as unruly as the Bedern. The Quakers, particularly, saw the violence around them as the result of booze, and to a great extent they were right (£60,000 a year, one journal reckoned, was spent on drink in the city). They brought into existence temperance organisations to combat the evil.

Like most radical movements, the temperance movement quickly split into warring elements—the believers in "temperance" and the advocates of "total abstinence." These two in York, as elsewhere, spent as much time and energy in attacking each other as they did attacking the drink interests. The older temperance organisation (the British and Foreign Temperance Society) was known as "The Old Moderation Society," and to Hopwood, for a time a secretary of the York Total Abstinence Society, "moderation" was "the cause of all drunkeness." His organisation was a large one that had opened a lecture hall in Goodramgate in 1845 which cost £1,500. The *Gazette* called Hopwood "a chartist" but there is no evidence that he was, though he was not beyond mixing (radical) politics in with his orations to "the aquatic fraternity."

Hopwood proposed Lowther from amongst the crowd. "The proceedings of the present election," he said, "forcibly remind me of the gloomy days of Old Sarum and Gatton . . . you all know as well as I do," he went on, "that our old and esteemed representative Mr. Lowther, has disappeared from amongst us in a very mysterious manner, and I know you will be told that Mr. Lowther will not stand a contest. Take my advice," he concluded, not very logically, "put him at the head of the poll, and he will stand." Lowther was seconded by F.E. Wilkinson, a schoolmaster. R.S. Lambert erroneously says that "a chemist named White" moved the "nomination of Sir John Lowther."

At this stage of the proceedings G.T. Andrews, "Hudson's cat's paw" asked Hopwood if he and Wilkinson were prepared to pay the expenses of going to a poll. Hopwood said that he was not, but that he would guarantee the amount needed. After a consultation with the Lord Mayor, Sheriff Andrews said he would not accept Hopwood's guarantee. Smythe and Yorke, he said, had both deposited £200 and despite (perhaps because of) Hopwood's protest that he expected two Lowther supporters who could produce the money to be present, Andrews would only allow five minutes for the money to be produced. When it was not forthcoming Hudson, as Mayor, announced Smythe and Yorke elected. An eye witness wrote afterwards that he "heard the burst of indignation with which this unjust decision was received, and read in that general execration the fate of that petty dynasty which would fain trample upon the rights and independence of the citizens of York." Thomas Wilson of Layerthorpe maintained that he had been outwitted. Wilson was a radical who said he had wanted to propose George Leeman, "but through the trickery of the Sheriff . . . had not had the opportunity of doing so." A handbill went the rounds of the city saying that a Captain Darnell and William Charles Anderson, a surgeon of Micklegate, would have produced the £200 had they been given time.

Hudson's catologue of mistakes was lengthening. At the beginning of the hustings he was unpopular; at the end he was hated—at least by large selections of the populace. He had denied "the venal freemen" of York an election, with all that implied in bribes and booze. To his lackeys, however, he was still the Railway King, and he lashed out furiously at his enemies. Simpson had, of course, nominated Yorke (and he may also have angered Hudson over the part he had played in a recent attempt to get a Bill to manage the strays), but it was only a few months since he had welcomed Hudson back to the city when the latter had won Sunderland for the Tories. Now he was "the little Knight. . . The Knight who proposed [Yorke] . . . in such flippant and unmeaning language that no one—not even himself . . . could understand the effect of it." Hopwood was "Mr. Teetotaller," a man who "had no right by property or position to interfere with the representation of York," and Wilkinson's financial position was not all that it might have been. The *Gazette* hinted that he was "of no extensive credit" and Hudson said he was "an individual [who] had just escaped from a neighbouring mansion, where, he had scheduled his debts. . . " Without money an individual had no rights in the Hudson scheme of things.

The Lord Mayor had drawn up a formidable opposition to himself in a few months—first were a few radicals; then a radical leader of heroic proportions had at last appeared to try a throw with a great man; then the populace at large had been aliented when he denied them an election. His treatment of Lowther had also angered a few members of his own party, and one of them joined forces with Hopwood and Wilkinson, to give the opposition something of the appearance of a popular front. This was the George White, chemist, of Heworth, mentioned by Lambert. White does not seem to have been a Peelite; he was secretary of the York Farmer's Club, and someone genuinely angered at the demonstration of bullying and arrogance the city had witnessed in recent times.

Hopwood, White, Wilkinson and others (not the official leaders of the Liberals) held huge protest meetings in the city. Hopwood told them of "the hand of tyranny" that was Hudson's and "the grossest act of injustice ever practised upon a free people." Hudson had referred to his calling, Hopwood said, but if the Railway King had been "a disciple of the pump" he might have been a better man —"on the floor of the British Senate, he is a mere buffoon; and in the railway world, so far as his influence extends, he is a tyrant and a traitor." Hopwood and his colleagues drew up a petition protesting against Smyth's election which was sent off for legal opinion. An election in Dublin, the *Yorkshireman* reported, had been held in which similar events to those in York had occurred, and an addition as a late candidate had been named. There the Sheriff had allowed time to get the deposit, and the last-named man had eventually won.

A committee was created to raise subscriptions to obtain a petition to unseat Smyth. What an extraordinary reversal of fortune. In 1835 the Liberals had petitioned to unseat Lowther, now they were preparing to petition again because he was ousted! The *Gazette* said that "Not a single person of character and influence [was] mixed up with" Hopwood's committee, and the Hargrove papers called them "low radicals" and Chartists. This was not true. Hopwood was the secretary of an organisation that had over 1,700 members, and White was also secretary of an influential group.

Among the others who were so contemptuously dismissed by the *Gazette* and whose names deserve recording were John Duncan, editor of the *Yorkshireman*; Richard Anderson, journeyman currier secretary of the York Working Men's Health of Towns Association; William McLaren, beer seller and a well-known radical; George Heineman, attorney; J. Smith, grocer of Bootham; William Snow, keeper of the famous Snow's Temperance Hotel, Low Ousegate; Samuel Gibson, wine and spirit merchant, Petergate; George Gibson, brewer of the City Brewery, Walmgate; Thomas Oates, hatter, Parliament Street.

None of the city's leading Liberals, except Duncan and Captain Darnell, were associated with Hopwood, nor any of the city's leading Quakers. George Leeman, James Meek and Joseph Rowntree, for example took no part in his campaign and their absence gives rise to speculation. Did they deliberately stay clear and give support behind the scenes, thinking that a grass roots opposition to Hudson would look better and would be more effective? Leeman eventually said that he was against the move to unseat Smyth on the very good grounds that, if successful, it would unseat Yorke also. Leeman did eventually lend his support to Hopwood, but the others remained aloof and deserve the criticisms of posterity for doing so. Hopwood always maintained that his movement was one of "no party"—but it might be worth recording that the *Gazette* was convinced that the Anti-Corn Law League was behind it, at least when it was directed at unseating Smyth.

In August Hopwood and White addressed a crowd of 5,000 in St. Sampson's Square. White attacked his one-time leader. "The same influence which had displayed itself on this occasion had been at work for many years. There had been bribery and corruption at work . . ." White said a committee to secure the freedom of election in the future would be set up. Hopwood told the crowd that he and his committee were receiving messages of support from other towns and that a requisition to Smyth had been drawn up asking him to resign which already had 1,000 signatures. It would have had more but Hudson had issued threats to his workmen.

"We have found", Hopwood said, "that in [York] there exists a power which exercises over the minds of many of the constituency a most debasing and unhallowed influence . . . a power and influence of the most degrading kind, it is a bread and cheese—a pounds, shillings, and pence influence that rules the people here . . . to be the slave of a man who has nothing to commend him to our esteem and affections—a man of purse-proud insolence and dominating spirit—is a position so miserably humiliating that I do most solemnly and deliberately declare that I would at once become a knight of the broom and sweep the streets of the city all the days of my life, rather than be willing to bow my neck beneath a bondage so vile as this."

The *Gazette* and the *Herald* practically ignored Hopwood's campaign, of course, which by late August he had decided to conduct on three fronts. A legal opinion had been received from Francis Newman Rogers saying that the election proceedings *were* illegal, and it was decided to go ahead with the petition to Parliament. It was also decided to press on with the requisition (to save time and money the *Yorkshireman* told Hudson to tell Smyth to apply for the Chiltern Hundreds and enable a bye election to take place). Then a head-on challenge to Hudson would be mounted at the municipal elections in November. Every ward represented by "Mansion House flunkeys" would be contested, regardless of the outcome of the action against Smyth. They were being constantly reminded of their ingratitude and of Hudson's improvements to the city, John Duncan told his readers. "Pray, what scheme of improvement has he ever embarked in, save for the personal profit of himself and his familiars," he added sarcastically.

In September the requisition, with 1,253 signatures, was taken to Smyth by a deputation. They were met by Smyth himself, and those two prominent Hudsonians, George Dodsworth and James Richardson. Smyth, not unexpectedly, refused to resign and asked that the requisition be left with him. Recognising that this would leave the door open to massive victimisation, Duncan refused, knowing he said that the *Gazette* and the *Herald* would misrepresent why. "He does the family washing of the occupant of the Mansion House," wrote Duncan referring to William Hargrove and his "recreant print," and went on, "we can easily pardon the amount of soap he uses, when we consider the extreme foulness of the materials he attempts to cleanse." Following Smyth's refusal, Hopwood and his friends said they would persist in the petition, and assured the Liberals that if Yorke, too, were unseated, he would be returned free of expense. Lowther would definitely stand, Hopwood assured the crowds. The possibility that Lowther himself was behind all the campaigning suggests itself, but is too remote to be credible. (He never made any pronouncement about what went on).

On 16 October the *Herald* reported that Hopwood, Duncan and the others, the "*self-elected guardians* of the city's interests" had met and drawn up a panel of candidates for the November elections. According to Hopwood, Barnabas ("Barabbas") Mitchell infiltrated the committee, and many of the attacks on their deliberations came from him and "that notorious [and anonymous] scribbler R.H. Anderson." Before the elections took place, George Leeman gave Hopwood his blessing. Leeman said he completely approved of the attempt to purge the council, if not that to unseat Smyth. About to retire were three Liberals (R.W. Hollon, Francis Calvert and W.P. Parkinson)and nine others—"as pretty a bunch of Hudsonian trucklers as could be gathered together."

They were John Cluderay, builder of Aldwark, a councillor for Monk since he had replaced Peter Rymer, deceased, at a bye election in 1841; Matthew Rymer also of Monk, coal merchant, first returned in 1844; William Hudson, proctor, and Thomas Hanley Barker, surgeon, the councillors for Bootham; R. H. Anderson; George Hutchinson, spirit merchant, of Walmgate, first returned in 1844; David Hill, currier, councillor for Walmgate since 1840; John Roper, brewer, Guildhall Ward, member of the council (with one tiny break) since its creation, and John Wilson, butcher, Roper's colleague in Guildhall, there since 1842.

The attack on Hudson had been mounted. Since the general election he had not appeared often in York, and it seemed almost certain that he would suffer a severe set-back. What took place was certainly the most exciting contest in York's municipal history. What took place will seem incredible to the modern reader. His back against the wall, a massive history of recent mistakes behind him, faced with able antagonists for the first time, Hudson was challenged head-on—*and he won every single seat*! He did it by the usual methods. He won even in a ward where, even in the great days, no Conservative had ever been returned. Hudson, it seemed, was unassailable.

EVEN with the tide flowing for them (apparently), the Liberals did not try to win in Bootham and Guildhall, the retiring Tory councillors there being returned unopposed. In Walmgate there was "a mock struggle" when John Wilberforce, a labourer, and George Wilson were put up as Liberals, but were easily beaten. They were beaten by "breakfasting" and boozing, but interest centred on the remaining three wards, where the really symbolic attacks on the Railway King were to take place.

In Castlegate that political maverick, Robert Henry Anderson, was up for re-election, as was his Liberal colleague Hollon. George Leeman, who had once worked for—and been sacked by—Robert Henry, was responsible for moving in George Peacock Bainbridge, woollen draper of Fishergate. This prompted sensation number one.

From small beginnings . . . Above: George Hudson's birthplace in the tiny village of Howsham on the edge of the Wolds near York. Below: Newby Hall (now Baldersby Park), near Thirsk, which Hudson bought from Earl de Grey in October 1845. He had to sell it in 1854.

Hudson's homes in York—1. College Street, showing on the left the
premises in which he lived and ran a draper's shop following his
marriage in 1821 to Elizabeth Nicholson, wife of a York solicitor.
Hudson later referred to this era as "the happiest part of my life."
(From a sketch made in 1932).

Hudson's homes in York—2. The town house, No. 44 Monkgate, into which he moved in 1827 on inheriting a fortune from his great-uncle, Matthew Bottrill. The building has recently been restored.

Hudson in stone. A bust now in York Railway Museum.

Hudson on canvas. An unsigned portrait of the Railway King now hanging in the Wear Commissioner's Offices at Sunderland. (British Railways).

Hudson stations. Above: View from the City Walls of the first York station which survived until the 1960s. Its opening on May 29th, 1839, provided Hudson with a welcome excuse for a great ceremony—a gargantuan breakfast, a $5\frac{1}{2}$ hour dinner and dancing until 4.0 a.m. Below: Monkwearmouth, on the north bank of the Wear, built in grandiloquent manner to symbolise the Railway King's associations with nearby Sunderland. (British Railways).

Unfulfilled hopes. Above: Imposing viaduct at Tadcaster, the only portion constructed of Hudson's Leeds–York direct line of 1846. Photographed in November 1964. (K. Miller). Below: Long avenue at Londesborough, photographed from the site of the private station which Hudson built on the York–Market Weighton line. His plans to establish a family seat at the end of this drive were dashed by his downfall.

Contemporary politicians. Top, left: A sketch of Hudson now displayed in York Railway Museum. Top, right: John Henry Lowther, Tory M.P. for York from 1835 to 1847. (from an election card, per York City Libraries). Right: George Leeman, Hudson's principle opponent in York. (from an illustration in "Vanity Fair").

The Conservatives in retaliation chose Bartholomew Thomas Wilkinson as Anderson's running mate. Now Wilkinson was a Hudsonian *par excellence*, manager of the York Union Bank, and one of the people who owed everthing to the great man. He was also, however, a servant of the city council. He was city treasurer and Leeman pointed out that, if elected, he could not sit, but that deterred no-one. "The railway is determined to have everybody in the council connected with the railway before it is done. It has got its chairman" Leeman said, "it has got several of its directors [Simpson, Thomas Barstow, Richardson, Dodsworth among them]—it has got the Town Clerk one of its directors—it will not rest until it has down to its very stokers."

Leeman was stung to his last remark as much by Wilkinson's nomination as by what had happened in Micklegate. This was the ward which had not had a Tory councillor since 1836, and which had gone unchallenged since 1840. William Pickering Parkinson had sat for Micklegate since 1841 and Francis Calvert, solicitor, since 1838. These two intended to seek re-election. The Calvert family had run into trouble over the management of the ward's strays and had fallen foul of Hudson who had taken differing views. So had that stormy petrel, R.H. Anderson. Francis Calvert was in the same line of business as Anderson, and the latter maintained that he and his brother, Edward Calvert, a pasture master, were lining their pockets. Rather worse, one of the Calverts had helped Leeman in pushing Bainbridge against Robert Henry in Castlegate. The latter retaliated—still masquerading as a "Liberal"—by spearheading a Tory foray into Micklegate.

There had been many demonstrations of Anderson's subservience by this time, notably the gleeful acceptance of the jibe that he wore the Railway King's livery, but few stood him in worse stead than the part he played in Micklegate in 1847. Anderson addressed meetings in the ward, cashed in on trouble over the strays, and urged electors to choose new candidates. Their choice fell on John Walton Nutt, comb maker of Trinity lane, and Thomas Cabrey. Both were Conservatives. The latter was the resident engineer of the York and North Midland Railway.

Immediately after the nomination of Cabrey and Nutt, money and beer began to flow. "Open houses" were kept for the thirsty and blatant intimidation was practised. Calvert and Parkinson began a canvass, but realised that their efforts were doomed to failure. They withdrew before polling day Micklegate "has quietly been given up to the railway interest," said the *Yorkshireman*, ". . . the recent growth of the railway interest in the ward rendered [Parkinson's and Calvert's] chances of being returned exceedingly problematical." The week before the elections were due it realised what was going to happen. "To have seen a Liberal ward entered by a *soi disant* Liberal, for the purpose of supporting two out and out Tories is an anomaly." Not in Hudson's York, though. Just what railway influence meant was revealed, in part, by Hopwood later. Talking about employment on the railway, he said, "It is all useless for an individual who is not either a freeman or a £10 householder to apply for employment."

In Monk, "the very heart of the Railway King's influence" and one of the poorest wards in the city, known sometimes as "Hudson's Bay," probably the greatest struggle in York municipal politics took place. Monk was the ward in which Hudson lived, and the ward he represented when a councillor himself (for the very short time before he was made an alderman). At the very first municipal elections the Liberals had gained four out of the six seats for Monk, but thereafter it solidly returned Conservatives. Cluderay and Rymer stood again in 1847, and they were opposed by none other than Frederick Hopwood.

Hopwood waged a superb campaign. "We hear on all sides," said the *Yorkshireman* in its last editorial before polling began, "that the partisans of Messrs. Cluderay and Rymer boast that they can *purchase* (*like cattle*) *the freeman and electors of Monk Ward* for half a crown." It reminded its readers of Hudson's disinterestedness in his dealings with the city. When the railway company wanted a station he paid £5,000 for the old House of Correction which had cost the city £30,000. When the gas company wanted land of his worth £2,000 he charged it £5,000! Now that Hudson had a monopoly (having got the Great North of England) the price of coal was going up.

Hopwood was defeated. He was defeated by bribery and intimidation on a grand scale. Richard Nicholson, Hudson's brother-in-law, a "pompous fragment of supercilious humanity" the *Yorkshireman* called him, went round the ward threatening tradesmen with a loss of patronage if they honoured their pledges to Hopwood. 270 plumpers were promised Hopwood in his canvass and 57 split votes, but only 261 were eventually recorded for him, 175 less than for the second Tory (Cluderay 450, Rymer 436, Hopwood 261). In a bitter speech at the conclusion of the contest Hopwood talked of how he had been beaten. He and his colleagues had no electoral experience, and they had not spent sixpence in influencing voters. But their opponents had. Bribery and drunkeness went on unchecked and many of those responsible were prominent Wesleyans! "The great promoters of drunkeness had been active in debasing their fellow-creatures, who the night before were groaning and bawling, and calling upon the Lord, in a chapel." He went on, "There were also the sturdy advocates of another sect, who must have got a dispensation to degrade and debase the people by bribing them." The "tyrant company," of course, had threatened its workers living in the ward. James Chadwick had actively "solicited" and "bribed" people, and, Hopwood said, "He knew that positive orders had been given by several masters, that if their men voted for him (Mr.H.) they should have the sack.

In Castlegate, Anderson and B.T. Wilkinson easily topped the poll. £1,000 had been spent to return them, the *Yorkshireman* said. Commenting on the overall results, Leeman reverted to an earlier theme. "Now the other day," he said, the railway company, in addition to its directors and "shareholders in abundance," "got its engineer" on the council, "so that it [now] has its lawyer [Richardson], its engineer [Cabrey], and now today it will have its banker." Anderson addressing the crowd at the declaration of the poll told them that all parties had "united in bearing their testimony and high approval of our very excellent Lord Mayor and his acts," and condemning "the acts and deeds of a set of persons you all well know after the apellation of Hopwood, White and Co."

Hopwood must have been staggered by the results of November 1847. Nothing, it must have seemed, could hurt Hudson; his position was impregnable; he could ride rough-shod over his party, his colleagues and his city at will. Hopwood said he would fight again; "he had their affections and . . . he would not part with them for the wealth of George Hudson," but John Duncan was bitterly, and perhaps unreasonably, hurt, bearing in mind how vulnerable the electorate were. "They had made an experiment in [Monk] as regarded principle, and he declared to the working men that he should hereafter be somewhat lukewarm . . . in their behalf. He declared that he should pledge himself not to work for them as had hitherto done. He had found the working men polling against them, although they had actually promised their votes. He had done fighting for them." The *Gazette* rubbed salt into the wounds of Leeman, Hopwood, White and the others:

"You have enjoyed the delight of Malvolio, for you have revelled in anticipated pleasures. Cheer up, though the delusion be passed; it was a pleasant dream; the castles of your pride have been crumbled to the dust; but you have had your delicious reverie, and one day of such enjoyments is worth an age of disappointments."

The Conservatives having taken all the seats, the boot was put in — Hudson fashion. The Tories could not punish Hopwood or Leeman, but they turned on the Liberal aldermen who had fallen from grace, in a time-honoured fashion. First of all they asked Hudson to accept office as Lord Mayor for a fourth time, but he refused. Then they chose Sir John Simpson, for so long a follower of the Railway King but now, for very little, out of favour. Simpson's crimes against Hudson seem slight, but he was elected in his absence. Simpson refused office and was fined, ". . . finding that the worthy knight had refused to become the "cat's paw" of the "Conservative body," it was resolved to punish him by electing him to the office, in order to

be enabled to enforce the required penalty of One Hundred Pounds."
Then James Meek got the same treatment and was fined. Finally,
and this seems appropriate in 1847, the council chose James Richardson, Hudson's solicitor and "man-of-all-work." Richardson had
been made an alderman in the place of Henry Cobb, who had stood
down, fearing he might be chosen as Mayor.

At the end of 1847, whatever the murmurings about him were
nationally, Hudson was more firmly entrenched in power in York
than ever. He had routed his enemies and the corporation was
equated with the railway company—with the city treasurer as a
councillor a final humiliation. The radicals lost heart, and in December the *Yorkshireman* announced that the Smyth petition was to
be abandoned for lack of funds. Its abandonment seemed to emphasise the inescapable reality of the Railway King's influence in
York.

EARLY in 1848 Henry Redhead Yorke committed suicide and a
bye-election had to take place. Hudson however was rarely in the
city during the year, and he took no part in the contest. 1848 was a
dreadful time for him, and R.S. Lambert deals at length with the
events of that awful year. Hudson was ill, and Robert Davies retired.
Lord George Bentinck, leader of the Conservatives who had drawn
Hudson into the inner circles of the party, and George Stephenson,
an important figure in Hudson's life, both died. Murmurings about
the King's railway dealings had begun in 1847 but in '48 revelations
of monumental peculation began to come to light. The Eastern
Counties Railway, of which Hudson had become chairman, ran into
difficulties and a dividend of only 8s. per £20 share was declared.
A slump set in on the shares of the other Hudson companies, and
by the last quarter of the year things were desperate. "Throughout
the first eight months of 1848 the premiums on ... shares [in the
Hudson lines] had been gradually melting away; still, up to the last
week in August, they all kept their heads near to, or above par. Then
the panic began." Day by day, an editorial in the *Yorkshireman*
recorded in October, things got worse in the railway market. York
and North Midland shares "have been sold at £41, being a discount
of £39; Midland Counties at £65 or at a discount of £35; Great
Western at £65½, or a £24½ discount; North British at £11. 5s., a
discount of £13. 15s., Lancashire and Yorkshire have fallen to £35
discount."

A week before the editorial quoted above appeared, the Lendal
bridge affair came to light again in York. An abstract of expenses
incurred in obtaining the Act was published, and it was seen that,
despite what Hudson had said, all charges had been made to the
city treasurer! (The sum was £2,377 14s. 9d.). The *Yorkshireman*

reminded its readers that the municipal elections were not far off (Duncan had regained some of his enthusiasm) and urged that there be another attempt to throw the Hudsonians out. The cholera was on the rampage and the council was under fire. Hudson's followers had made no arrangements to fight the plague, and already people had succumbed to its ravages.

Yet in spite of all this it seems that an arrangement was entered into between the "old Whigs" and the Conservatives by which all the retiring councillors were to be allowed walk-overs (8 Conservatives, 4 Liberals). But the more radical section of the Liberal party refused dictation from above and a series of contests did take place.

Edward Calvert, hated by the Tories, was to retire for Castlegate and sought re-election. Unable to resist an attempt to oust him, the Conservatives started George Brown, draper, of High Ousegate, and so were guilty of a "scandalous breach of faith." It seems fantastic that such an agreement could have been entered into, but the starting of Brown freed those Liberals who were prepared to honour it (the *Gazette* admitted that it was a purely personal opposition). In Guildhall, William Fox, Leeman's partner, and William Sotheran were put up to fight Henry Bellerby and Husband, "two of the most unscrupulous partizans of Mr. Hudson," and Bellerby and Husband were beaten.

Candidates were also introduced into Hudson's Monk Ward. Joseph Hunt finished only nine votes behind Jethro Heseltine, the second Tory. With a proper ward organisation it could have been won. As it was, the *Yorkshireman* said, the result showed that it "is now emancipated from the hitherto overwhelming influence of Mr. Hudson." That was a wild charge, but in Castlegate Edward Calvert and his colleague shook off the Tory challenge. Rather more important, this year there was no challenge to the Liberals in Micklegate. They seemed to have learned their lesson about electoral methods. (The "Huntonians" were said to have "treated" in Monk and in Guildhall—where Bellerby took his defeat with very bad grace — the Liberals were also supposed to have dispensed food and drink). The Tories were unsure of themselves. Their leader was absent from the city, busy trying to salvage his lines and his reputation. He was still believed in in York, but his minions lacked his guiding genius. Yet they still had a majority of 19, at least, on the council.

The Liberals were delighted with the results of 1848. All the ballyhoo of 1847 had ended in disaster. Now, because of Tory vindictiveness towards Calvert, much more had been achieved. The defeat of Bellerby was regarded as a great victory, a portent. "The political engineers of His Railway Majesty, have, this week, been hoisted with their own petards," The *Herald* applauded Clark and Sotheran's victory in Guildhall as "a great moral victory . . . Toryism," it went on, "is evidently on the decline—a re-action is taking place . . . the corporation . . . will be reformed." Hargrove had read the signs and was on the way back to his earlier allegiances and cutting free from Hudson. The *Yorkshireman* also looked to the future. "Let us try, whether . . . we cannot emancipate the city from the thraldom of railway Directors and railway porters." There was talk of fighting every seat in 1849. "The task," of emancipating York, "we conceive, is an easy one, and we shall take care that it is not lost sight of." An easy task! The *Yorkshireman*'s sentiments make a fantastic comparison with Duncan's gloom of a year earlier.

A very significant breach *had* been made in the Hudson monopoly, it is true. But during 1848, when the Railway King had his back against the wall, people still believed in him in his own city. Hudson retained his popularity there long after he lost it in most places. Many more revelations had to come before he fell from grace in York. This might be illustrated by two instances. In April 1849 William Etty, the city's other favourite son, said he was willing to pledge his whole "existence on the honour and honesty of George Hudson," and when the council met for the first time in November 1848 Robert Henry Anderson, as he had done once before, raised the question of the charges for the Lendal Bridge Act. Robert Henry was as satisfied with Hudson's assurances that the railway's obligations would be met then, as he had been three years earlier.

Etty lived to see his hero destroyed. Throughout 1849 more and more revelations of Hudson's dealings came to light. Money had been used to bribe MPs. Hudson had made large profits selling his own companies. The *Yorkshireman* declared it intended to harry "the doomed Sardinapulus of Railways" to the end—he would be forced to disgorge his money and would not suffer alone, "Mr. Hudson shall have companions in his seclusion at Newby Hall, and when he falls, he falls not alone." One by one he resigned his chairmanships, and Meek and Joseph Rowntree were among those who replaced him, Barstow and Richardson on the board of the York and North Midland. Leeman became secretary and eventually deputy chairman of another Hudson company. In July the Railway King resigned as a director of the York Union Bank; two months earlier Richard Nicholson, his brother-in-law, unable to face the dreadful revelations of dividends out of capital, bribes and sharp practice as they came out, committed suicide. Hudson's life was in ruins. He was forced to put up houses and estates for sale, for which, the *Northern Star* said, he had paid "within a trifle of £700,000." This prompted a sarcastic little comment from the *Yorkshireman*:

> "Mr. HUDSON'S DELINQUENCIES—A great railroad man reading the other day the amount of money invested in landed property (now announced for sale) by Mr. Hudson, exclaimed, "Seven hundred thousand pounds! What an infernal rascal! I have not cleared seventy thousand."

York was shocked as the incontrovertable evidence of Hudson's pecadilloes came out. In June Leeman and his friends were able to cash in on the Tories' embarrassment. W.S. Clark resigned as an alderman and was replaced by G.H. Seymour, a Liberal. (Unsure of themselves, the Tories had also chosen a Liberal Lord Mayor). Seymour was a councillor for Micklegate and, as was almost inevitable, was replaced by Francis Calvert, ousted in the devastation of 1847. The Tories were still secure in control of the corporation, but their numbers were being whittled away. Hudson was rarely present after the first few months of 1849 and B.T. Wilkinson left the city. Now Clark had gone, and Francis Calvert was back. Things looked set for a great Liberal effort and victory in November. They were helped by revelations of jobbing on the Hudson council that came out in September.

John Pulleyn was the city surveyor and the finance committee of the corporation had ordered him to issue specifications for contracts to repair corporation houses in New Street. The lowest tender was accepted, but the word went round that Pulleyn's son had been paid £30 for erecting scaffolding on the site. Pulleyn had employed his son—and the son was in partnership with him! The *Herald*, now with its anti-Hudson bias, shouted that here was evidence of Hudsonian corruption. (Pulleyn was a conservative it seems almost too obvious to point out). The son had done work before for the council. "Pulleyn and his son have been on the habit of doing the Corporation's work, which had afterwards to be surveyed and pronounced satisfactory—by whom?—why by Mr. Pulleyn himself!!!" The *Herald* demanded Pulleyn's dismissal, and he was eventually called before the council and questioned. The finance committee were ordered to prepare a report on the charges against the surveyor.

All this was a great propaganda for the Liberals. Preparations began for the elections earlier than ever before. "Late events," the *Gazette* said, "have encouraged our opponents to come forward and endeavour again to monopolize the municipal representation." George Leeman masterminded the operation, and Leeman was presented, by his enemies, as someone hankering after something like Hudson's absolutism. An equal number of Tories and Liberals were retiring, and, said the *Yorkshireman*, "There must be no compromise with any member of Hudson's tribe." Earlier it had declared that Hudson had "been formerly proclaimed as unworthy," and his creatures, who had been "foisted upon the different wards by Hudson . . and his badged band of hangers-on" should be forced to "suffer the penalty thereof."

Interest in 1847 had centred on Micklegate, the Liberal stronghold the Railway King took over in his great demonstrations of power. In 1849 interest centred on Bootham, where Tory walkovers had occurred in 10 out of 14 elections since 1836, and where "to even suggest a contest [has been] considered an absurdity."

There in 1849 John Walker and Henry Newton were due to retire and Walker did not seek re-election. The Conservatives chose none other than W.D. Husband to replace him. It was a great mistake.

Husband was the man turned out of Guildhall, along with Bellerby, in the Liberal revival of 1848. No more dyed-in-the-wool Hudsonian could have been found: ". . . a man . . . in season, and out of season," Husband had "invariably defended and apologised for Mr. Hudson on every possible occasion." Husband was always first in the queue to compliment or applaud the Railway King, was a regular attender at council meetings, and had the reputation of being a windbag. ". . . he thought himself," the *Herald* said, "the mouthpiece of the Corporation Tories, but his tedious harangues 'solemn and slow,' on the most trifling of subjects, will long be remembered as the feeble efforts of *superogation*, more pleasing to himself than instructive to those around him." Husbands' "servility" according to John Duncan, was "a matter of public notoriety."

Husband's running mate was even more obviously a Hudson man. Henry Newton was another Railway Solicitor, who had been mixed up with Mr. Hudson's acts of embezzlement." Hudson had registered shares in Newton's name, and although it was established that Newton had complained about it, he had nevertheless signed the transfers and was compromised. ". . . no more unpopular men," in 1849, "could have been selected by the Tories than Mr. Newton and Mr. Husband."

The Liberals nominated two candidates for Bootham—James Meek junior, and James Allen, a surgeon. Canvassing and electioneering, and, according to both sides, bribery and intimidation went on for almost a month. That well-established practice of "hocussing" also went on; one man was treated to Richmond races, and another sent on a spurious errand into the West Riding. Newton and Husband were sensationally defeated. They were beaten by the revulsion of feeling against their fallen, crooked leader, and the votes of men "smarting under railway losses." It would be revealing to know what those losses actually amounted to. Hudson's estimates of investment and income have been quoted earlier.

If Bootham could be won, so surely could the rest of the seats· Even in this year, however, Monk was beyond the Liberals' grasp· Although they had whittled the Conservative majority down to 12, there was still a long way to go. If the Tories purged themselves completely of Hudson, they reckoned *they* might still hang on to power. Conditions would never, surely, be as favourable to the Liberals as they had been in 1849. When the new council met for the first time, Hudson's final humiliation—at the hands of erstwhile worshippers—began.

IT was clearly Tory voters who had ousted Newton and Husband in Bootham. As soon as it was proved that Hudson was down, men admitted his failings and deserted him—but not until it was quite clear that he could not revive his fortunes. In 1847 men could read what he was like—but in York they ignored what they read. So too in 1848. In 1849 however the rush to denounce the fallen King was disgusting.

The Tories chose George Hicks Seymour, Liberal, Justice of the Peace, lawyer, chairman of the City Improvement Commission and now deputy chairman of the York and North Midland, as Lord Mayor. But this time it was a conciliatory move, not an exercise in humiliation as the choice of Simpson had been. Seymour was proposed by Alderman Gray—who then went on to move that Hudson's aldermanic seat be declared vacant. Gray was seconded by John March, one of the new Conservative councillors, and Hudson was duly expelled. Alderman Matterson, the Wesleyan Mayor of Hudson's time, under whom the awful Victorian Sunday made great strides in York, proposed that B. T. Wilkinson's seat also be declared vacant. It was, and T. Craven, the confectioner, was chosen to replace him without opposition. The Liberals had made yet another gain.

Who was to replace Hudson as an alderman? "The Aldermanic gown was hawked round the city, but no-one would touch it. It seemed to carry about it a portion of the infamy of its former wearer." Nevertheless, it eventually found an owner, Henry Newton, Hudson's partner in shady dealings and the Conservative who had actually lost in Bootham. The gown had "found a consistent possessor", the *Yorkshireman* said. The office of alderman was now "a refuge for the destitute" according to George Leeman. Bringing in Newton was in bad taste, an error of judgement of the kind the York Tories in those bad days seemed unable to avoid. Newton was also the man associated with Husband, the person who had "attached to him the blot of having glozed, and fawned, and flattered in the council chamber."

Hudson's fall from grace was not yet complete. Matterson proposed "that the portrait of Mr. George Hudson be removed from the Mansion House." Matterson's motion was lost by only two votes, after Simpson, Leeman and others abstained. "A more scorching humiliation was never inflicted upon man." Later in the year the Railway King's effigy was "removed from his throne at Madame Tussaud's, and put in the melting pot," making wonderful copy for *Punch*. (Lambert's book contains a surprising error wherein he says that the portrait reproduced facing page 200—also included in this book (page 53)—is the one referred to above, hanging in the York Mansion House. That in the Mansion House is of Hudson in aldermanic robes standing before a table on which York's ceremonial sword and mace are lying. It is completely different from Lambert's illustration, the original of which, in fact, is in the Wear Commissioners' offices in Sunderland. There it is the largest in a large collection, and the only one unnamed and uncredited. The offices also contain two excellent oil paintings of Hudson opening the Sunderland Docks in 1850).

James Chadwick, Wesleyan, chairman of the York United Gas Light Company, and councillor for "Imperial Monk" was another who turned viciously on his fallen leader. In the new council Leeman moved that the bye law enabling the secret nomination of committees, a great feature of the Hudson system, be rescinded. Leeman was supported by Chadwick, and E. R. Anderson (R. H's brother) sarcastically told the council how pleasing it was to see Chadwick appearing in a new guise, as "one of the best reformers" on it. Leeman referred to the way committees had been packed under Hudson. Ten out of the eleven members of the all-important finance committee were aldermen, and only one (Simpson) was a Liberal. On the Ouse Navigation Committee the same predominance of Conservatives and aldermen had existed. Matterson joined with Leeman and Chadwick. "I was one of the Watch Committee," he said, "but because I could not chime in with them and spend my money in drunkeness and dissipation at municipal elections, they kicked me out . . . and six of George Hudson's flunkies signed a round robin against me." Matterson did not say how he squared his conscience and accepted office as alderman and Lord Mayor in such a dreadful regime, nor why he waited until Hudson had fallen before he spoke out.

Shortly afterwards, Matterson, stalking his prey like a hunter, found another opportunity to vent his spleen when an incident occurred which illuminated the Hudson system and the jobbing that was such a prominent feature of it. Robert Davies had retired and an attempt was made "to foist" William Benson Richardson, "a young man still in his articles" and the son of Alderman Henry Richardson (an ex Lord Mayor), into "the office of Clerk of the Peace for the City of York." Matterson was outraged and Robert Henry Anderson said the candidacy was an insult to the legal profession. Eventually the office was amalgamated with that of Town Clerk and the post went to Henry Richardson, James Richardson's brother. Years before James had demanded that the Clerk's salary be docked by £60 a year, but said nothing of this kind when his brother was the person involved. The *Yorkshireman* was delighted at the outcome: ". . . one of those scandalous jobs the Hudson faction has, of late years, been accumstomed to perpetrate, was signally frustrated."

1849 was the last year in which George Hudson himself played a part in York politics. There was no comeback. *Punch* adapted a poem of Cowper (The Royal George was a famous wreck):

TOLL for a knave
A knave whose day is o'er!
All sunk—with those who gave
Their cash, till they'd no more.

Toll for the knave!
The Royal GEORGE is gone
His last account is cook'd;
His work of doing, done!

HUDSON had gone, but his party was still in power in York. Friends of his who once hung on every word he uttered were vying with each other to purge themselves to save something of their careers. But they still had a majority on the council. And the city was to hear more still of the fiddles that went on in the Hudson years, before they were ousted.

In the last few years there have been moves to rehabilitate Hudson. They echo in some ways an attempt to do the same thing in the 1850s— this one stage managed, and paid for, by the great man himself. It arose out of an action in which James Richardson sued the *Yorkshireman* for libel. Hudson had resigned as director of the York Union Bank and at the end of January published a long manifesto to the shareholders of one of his companies attempting to defend himself against some of the grosser charges of which he had been found guilty. A little later the *Yorkshireman* produced an account of an annual general meeting of the bank which showed that one of Hudson's minions had been engaged in shady dealings on a grand scale. B.T. Wilkinson, the city treasurer whom Hudson had forced on York as a councillor while bringing the city to heel in 1847, had got his money mixed up with the bank's. Wilkinson was its manager, it will be remembered, and he had resigned "having overdrawn to the 'tune' of some £20,000 or thereabouts." Wilkinson had been speculating (on the railways) with bank funds. James Richardson had been attorney to the bank. "It certainly would appear," Duncan's paper said, "as if there existed a charter for mismanagement, artifice, and defalcation, in every joint-stock company over which Messrs. G. Hudson and James Richardson have had control." This was the libel complained of. The *Yorkshireman* had to prove fair comment, and the trial brought the fallen Railway King again to the city he was now said to have dishonoured.

It commenced in July 1850. Sergeant Charles Wilkins who had appeared in York as a pseudo-radical candidate in the election of 1848 represented the *Yorkshireman*. His brilliant speech ought to be required reading for those who believe Hudson should be honoured. Wilkins called the Railway King "the greatest enemy of mankind of his day . . . one who has brought about more desolation, has effected more misery, and has produced more ruin, than any man of his age . . . a stain upon the land—a blot on the commercial honour of the nation." Wilkins backed up his rhetoric with cold facts. He established that James Richardson "for his own purposes . . . [had] assisted Hudson in blinding and hoodwinking the public, and in leading them into the many delusions into which they were led." B.T. Wilkinson was a creature of Hudson's. He had been a second clerk in another bank before being made the manager of the Union, and Hudson knew about all his private investments. In the classic fashion Wilkinson had tried to retrieve the loss of a few thousands by massive speculation and got deeper and deeper into trouble. Wilkins asked him

> "Were there auditors at that bank?—There were no auditors.
> Were you, in 1846, trafficking in shares?—Yes.
> That, I suppose, would be known to Mr. Hudson?—Yes."

Before Hudson himself appeared in court it was revealed that it was none other than the vindictive Matterson who had let the cat out of the bag about what had gone on at the annual general meeting of the Union Bank. Matterson was a shareholder, and he had raised the question of Wilkinson banking with his own bank—and being sensationally in the red. It was Matterson who had given the *Yorkshireman* the details of the meeting that constituted the alleged libel.

Hudson was questioned by the Sergeant. Wilkinson had been a clerk earning £150 a year before his appointment at the Union, at a salary that eventually reached £1,000. By 1845 "he was a man worth fifteen or twenty thousand pounds . . ." Wilkins took Hudson through many of his major ventures, going over ground covered by committees of investigation but a short time earlier: the appropriating for himself of 2,000 new shares in the York and North Midland in 1846; how he took huge sums to pay landowners and pocketed them; how he bought iron rails at £12 a ton and sold them to his companies at a profit of £38,000. The jury found the libel not proved, but it was an expensive victory for Duncan and his colleagues.

The *Yorkshireman* produced a pamphlet-account of the trial that was widely noticed. At the same time another appeared favourable to Hudson written by William Digby Seymour, the barrister son of Hudson's agent in Sunderland. The pamphlet was one attempt among many of the time purporting to believe Hudson had gone a long way to exonerating himself by his York court appearance. The *Gazette* wrote in this way, and *John Bull* talked about Hudson's "perfect integrity in all his dealings"!! The *Sun*, the *Morning Chron-*

icle, the *St. James Chronicle* and the *Standard* all carried articles which the *Yorkshireman* said were attempts at "washing the black-a-more white."

Just who masterminded the white-washing operation became clear when John Henry Doyle, a proprietor of the *Weekly Chronicle* appeared in bankruptcy proceedings. Doyle had been proprietor, editor, publisher and printer of the *Chronicle* since July 1849, and he had been urged to publish the contents of Seymour's pamphlet. He had reluctantly agreed and a note of it had appeared in the review columns in September 1850.

Then he had been asked to publish a second Seymour article, "a most fulsome paregyric upon Mr. George Hudson." Doyle said that he "refused to allow the *Weekly Chronicle* to be corrupted" by defending the Railway King, and refused bribes of £100. His refusal cost him dear. The bankruptcy proceedings, brought by Edward Russell, a Hudson front man, were the direct result of it. Under new management the *Chronicle* became pro-Hudson. Doyle was another victim of Hudson's vindictiveness.

The proceedings against the *Yorkshireman* were gone through yet again, with the same result. Duncan said they were started to break his paper, started by that "dishonest Railway *Camarilla* panting for revenge because we had exposed their frauds, their cunning 'dodges,' and the discreditable practices they practiced on the nation." The Hudsonians had seized the first opportunity they got of paying back that paper which had been snarling incessantly at their heels since 1845 or '46. Although it got the verdicts, the *Yorkshireman* was saddled with heavy costs, costs it could ill afford. But it lived to see the final dismantling of the Hudson system in its city.

A T the beginning of 1850 another scandal exposing Jonathan Pulleyn, already under a cloud for his activities as city surveyor, was a blow to the Conservaties, anxious now to rid themselves of the Hudson image. As senior pasture master for Bootham he had given orders to build a bridge, and drain and level parts of the stray, and had "employed his own men and paid his own bills." The attack on Pulleyn was led by Michael Charlton, a Bootham pasture master and a prominent Liberal. Pulleyn was found guilty on many counts: he had overcharged; created work for his horses and carts when normally they would have been idle; and charged for the labour of one of his men when that man was appearing before the magistrates. Pulleyn had also obtained goods at discount, but the full cost had appeared in the strays accounts. "Some parties boldly hinted that Mr.Pulleyn had considered the percentage *as a perquisite of office*, which he promptly denied; but when asked if he would have done so

with his own accounts, he very coolly replied, 'That's a different
thing.'' One of the other pasture masters said the work done was
shoddy and a third compared Pulleyn to his erstwhile party boss.
"He had complained to Mr. Pulleyn of his conduct," he said,
"telling him he was proceeding in a course very similar to that of
Mr. George Hudson." Pulleyn was not re-elected.

A month later the Finance Committee of the Corporation reported
its investigations into Pulleyn's behaviour as city surveyor. As might
have been expected, the report contained only a mild condemnation
of Pulleyn's behaviour, but the case was proved according to John
Walton Nutt—the Tory foisted by Hudson on Micklegate in the
Liberal debâcle of 1847. ". . . the matter stood thus . . .," Nutt said

> "the finance committee desired Mr. Pulleyn to get contracts for certain work
> to be done in New Street. Mr. Pulleyn summoned half a dozen persons to
> send in tenders; he also offered a tender which was made the basis of their
> tenders by the other parties, and it was no matter whether it was for £5 or £50,
> rather than run the risk of offending Mr. Pulleyn they made theirs according
> to his."

Later in the year, the Corporation, with extended duties now, needed a new surveyor, and on 3 September decided to advertise for one.
James Chadwick, still full of righteous indignation, hinted that
there had been corruption over the valuation of properties in
Hudson's time—then went on to try and fix the appointment of a
surveyor, or so the Liberals said. Chadwick wanted to make a
full-time appointment but it was decided to advertise the post at
£200 and make it part-time. It was duly advertised and there were
29 applicants. When the council met in October to consider them,
Chadwick again tried to make the post full-time and overturn the
council's earlier decision. To make a full-time post, the *Herald*
said, with someone adequately qualified, would cost between £500
and £1,000 a year, but Chadwick maintained there were plenty of
persons able and willing to do the work full-time at £200. Chadwick
was supported by the rump of the old Hudson party—James Richardson, Cabrey, Newton and others. Immediately Leeman accused
them of "an artful dodge," an attempt to get the vitally important
job for a favourite (Conservative) candidate. "A youth without
experience, and without any practice to lose, would no doubt have
been elected," commented the *Herald*. Chadwick's move was defeated and J.B. Atkinson was elected. The Tories did not use their
majority to force the issue. Atkinson was unopposed, although a
Liberal nominee.

One by one revelations of sharp practice and corruption had
followed Hudson's own disgrace. B.T. Wilkinson had been shown to
have run his bank in the way his master ran his railways and his city.
The attempt to foist W.B. Richardson, an articled clerk, on the city
as clerk of the peace was a piece of flagrant jobbing, quite in keeping

with the way Hudson had behaved over Lendal Bridge, the dismissal of Lowther and the elections of 1847. The revelations of Pulleyn's activities showed a civic official blatantly manipulating contracts to suit himself. Finally, just a month before the municipal elections, James Chadwick had tried to repeat the Richardson exercise and plant a party nominee into the important post of surveyor. Hudson had gone but his party were still in power and it was plain to see they were adhering to the old methods. Prospects of seizing control of the city after a decade and a half in the wilderness looked better for the Liberals than ever they could have hoped. The scandals helped them, but of greater help was the fact that in 1850 those councillors so sensationally returned in 1847 were up for re-election (11 Conservatives, 1 Liberal). And aldermanic elections were due immediately after the elections.

The Liberals won eight out of the 12 seats, a gain to them of seven. They now, at last, had a majority of two (25 : 23) and the Hudson clique were finally out of power. A show of liberality was made in choosing the aldermen, and only half the seats were taken by the party now in power. George Leeman was elected, and so too, strange to relate, was R.H. Anderson. Two bye-elections were caused by the aldermanic elections and, when they were over, the Liberals were in power with a majority of six (27 : 21). The era of Hudson had ended, that of George Leeman was about to begin.

George Leeman went on to great things. He became an important railwayman himself (he had an enviable reputation as a railway lawyer by the mid-forties); he became, like Hudson, three times Lord Mayor of York and represented the city in Parliament. When he retired, his son succeeded him as a York MP. Leeman died in Scarborough in 1882, at the age of 73.

Leeman died lauded and honoured. His old adversary lived out the last years of his life in obscurity, deserted by his friends. Towards the end of 1871 he was taken ill in York and died in London on 14 December. He is buried in the little village of Scrayingham in East Yorkshire. Few colleagues from his great days accompanied him from York to his last resting place. Two who did were Cabrey and J.L. Foster of the *Gazette*. Also present was the doctor who attended him in his last illness—William Matterson, son of that doctor of the same name who had turned so savagely on Hudson when he was in trouble, and when it was safe to do so.

The extent to which Hudson was followed by the business and professional people in York should have been clear from the narrative, and some estimates (from Hudson himself) have been given of the holding of shares in his companies in York and its neighbourhood. Even allowing for exaggeration, there must have been severe setbacks for many investors when the crash came, although the true extent will probably never be known. Subscription lists from the very earliest days of the York and North Midland are in

existence, but they are not a guide to what happened at the end of
of the 40s. Many people, like Meek, sold their shares and they
would have changed hands many times before Hudson fell, in all
probability. One who did suffer was John Ford, the headmaster of
Bootham School. He confided in his diary:

> "11 mo. 27—Within this year [1849] my property has been reduced (by the
> Railway delinquencies of—) by more than half: but I can truly and thank-
> fully say, I have been freed from all pain or anxiety about it. We have unitedly
> sought for a thankful spirit for what is left. . . ."

The Brontë sisters also suffered. Charlotte revealed that Emily and
Ann were shareholders in the York and North Midland in a letter
written in the mid-forties, and spoke deprecatingly of them (they
had also subscribed to the Hudson testimonial). In 1849 it appeared
that by then she had become a shareholder herself, her misgivings
about the Railway King having been overcome. She described her
misfortunes with the same kind of phlegmatic detachment that Ford
affected

> ". . . the little railway property I possessed, according to original prices, formed
> already a small competence for me, . . . Now scarcely any portion of it can,
> with security, be calculated upon. I must . . . wait patiently till I see how
> affairs are likely to turn. . . . However the matter may terminate, I ought
> perhaps to be rather thankful than dissatisfied. When I look at my own case,
> and compare it with that of thousands besides, I scarcely see room for a
> murmur. Many, very many, are by the late strange railway system deprived
> almost of their daily bread. Such, then, as have only lost provision laid up for
> the future should take care how they complain".

Thomas Carlyle, in one of his *Latter Day Pamphlets*, writing of
the people who followed the Railway King, loosed his arrows of
sarcasm at those who believed his promises of increased dividends
overnight. People like James Chadwick, businessmen themselves,
who should have realised that Hudson's methods were dubious
allowed themselves, it is incredible to recall, to be steamrollered
out of ever questioning Hudson's methods. In 1849 it was established
beyond doubt that the York and North Midland books had been
"cooked" for years to produce Chadwick and his friends their ten
per cent. Their motive was greed, greed of the kind Logan Pearsall
Smith wrote about,

> "I am in his paid service, and reject none of the doles of his bounty, I too
> dwell in the House of Mammon. I bow before the Idol, and taste the Un-
> hallowed ecstacy."

Punch, which, like Carlyle, was sympathetic to Hudson when he
first fell, published a stanza in which the relations of John Bull
"with humbugging promoters" is hit off.

> "Said John, "Your plan my mind contents,
> I'm sick and tired of Three per cents;
> And don't get enough by my paltry rents—
> So he got hooked in by the railway "gents"."

Punch devoted a tremendous amount of space to the "universal
epidemic" that was the railway mania of the forties. In the mid
forties Mr. Punch drew up his "Rules and Regulations for Rail-

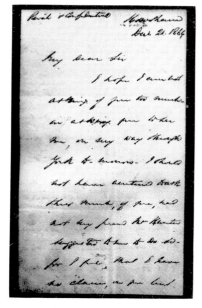

Hudson—understandably—committed little in writing, and the examples on this page are some of the very few that remain. Above: Letter written in commanding tones in August 1842. Below: Letter of December 1864 in more pleading style. (British Transport Historical Records).

Cheques to the Duke of Norfolk and Robert Stephenson, signed by Hudson for the Midland Railway. (British Transport Historical Records).

THE RAILWAY JUGGERNAUT OF 1845

Above: The Railway Mania as seen by Leech in *Punch*. Right: Hudson's rise and fall as depicted by "Crowquill." (a selection from "How He Reigned and How He Mizzled—A Railway Raillery"). Below: Map showing the relation of the North Midland and York & North Midland lines to the Leeds and Selby Railway (see pages 86—88).

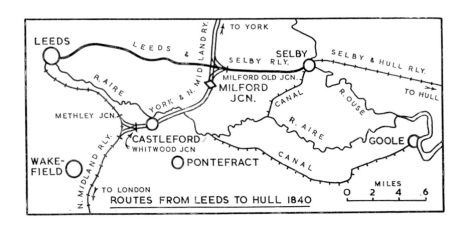

ROUTES FROM LEEDS TO HULL 1840

He shuts & cuts the shop | His success makes him jump for joy | He speaks in Public!!! | Every one will walk with him

He shows the Queen how to manage a Train | He does an extraordinary number of Lines!! | He is crowned!! The world is at his feet

He is Telegraphed for—It is stopped by his breeches pocket | Public confidence is shaken "Small profits but quick returns" | The Fiend deserts him!

· A · RAYLWAYE · MEETYNGE ·   EMOTYON · OF · Yᵉ · SHAREHOLDERES · AT · Yᵗ · ANNOVNCEMENTE · OF · A · DIVIDENDE · OF · 2¼ ·/₄

Hudson's downfall, through the eyes of *Punch*. In the evocative cartoon above the Railway King is presumably the figure at the extreme left on the platform. *Punch* accompanied the "Great Railway Guy" cartoon with some devasting verse:

Rotten now is his credit, as the fabric that fed it;
Out at elbows in character, credit and cash,
Like a GUY he is fleered at, and scouted and jeered at,
And all that he's good for's squib-firing and smash.

THE GREAT RAILWAY GUY FOR 1849.

PUNCH, OR THE LONDON CHARIVARI.

CELEBRATED COMIC SCENE BETWEEN THE RAILWAY CLOWN (Hudson) AND THE INDIGNANT SHAREHOLDERS.

DINNER IN THE GUILDHALL, YORK.

THURSDAY, DECEMBER 17th, 1846.

The Right Hon. George Hudson, M.P.,

LORD MAYOR.

SOUPS.

TURTLE.   HARE.
OX TAIL.   GRAVY.

FISH.

TURBOTS WITH LOBSTER SAUCE.
COD WITH OYSTER SAUCE.
WHITINGS.
HADDOCKS.
SMELTS.
SOLES.
FILLETS OF SOLES,
SALMON.
DOREY.

ENTREES.

CUTLETS OF MUTTON.
FILLETS OF PHEASANTS.
FILLETS OF PARTRIDGES.
CUTLETS OF PORK.
OYSTER PATTIES.
FRICASSEES OF CHICKEN.
VEAL, &c.

RELEVES.

HAUNCHES OF VENISON.
NECKS OF VENISON,
GAME PIES.
HAMS—TONGUES.
ROASTED PIGS.
ROASTED FOWLS.
BOILED FOWLS.
ROASTED TURKEYS.
BOILED TURKEYS.
ROASTED GEESE.
ROASTED DUCKS.
LEGS OF PORK.
DISHES OF VEGETABLES, &c.

GAME.

WOODCOCKS.
BLACK GAME.
PHEASANTS.
PARTRIDGES.
HARES.
WILD DUCKS.
SNIPES.

JELLIES.

NOYAU.
FRUIT.
MARASCHINO
MADEIRA WINE.
EAU DE VIE.

CREAMS.

VANILLE.
STRAWBERRY.
APRICOT.
ITALIAN.
MARBLE.

SALADS.

LOBSTER.
SHRIMP.
CHICKEN.
SAVOURY.

PASTRY.

TARTS.
FRUIT PIES.
MINCE PIES.
PLUM PUDDINGS, &c., &c.

DESSERT.

PINES, GRAPES, ORANGES, APPLES, DRIED FRUITS, CAKES, &c., &c.

Hudson sidelights. Left: Mouth-watering menu for a Hudson dinner held at York Guildhall on December 17th, 1846. To today's so-called affluent society, it seems almost unbelievable. (now in the possession of Mr. W. H. Hudson of York). Above, left: Carving set presented to the Railway King, showing his profile on the ivory handles and a train on the knife blade. (now in the possession of Mr. Henry Hudson of York). Above, right: One of Hudson's nicknames was "the royal railway stag." This view shows the stag which still stands outside his former London residence at Albert Gate. (R.D. Barrett–Lennard).

Back to the soil. The family grave in which George Hudson is buried at Scrayingham, then the church for Howsham.

"The graves were renovated in 1935 by members of the Hudson family and a few admirers of Geo. Hudson, known as the Railway King. . . ."

ways" one of which stated that

"No railway dividends to exceed 100 per cent,
and no bonus to be divided oftener than once a month."

He suggested a Joint Stock Railway Workhouse as the logical and
fitting end of the mania. It can be argued that the investors who
suffered when Hudson fell and the mania came to an end deserve no
more sympathy than they got from Carlyle and Smiles, but their
suffering is ignored in the attempt to rehabilitate him. More sympathy should be saved for the small shop keeper who did as the great
man bid, the workman who voted as he was told, the chapelgoer who
was forced to do violence to his conscience and take part in the electioneering described by Frederick Hopwood. It would be wrong to
suggest that the techniques used by Hudson were unique in Victorian England. They were not, but the degree to which they were
used bids fair to be unique. Certainly they were never used more
vindictively. Two years after he disappeared from the York scene
a general election took place. Voting was still public and poll books
were still published for contemporaries to see how their neighbours
voted. At the election, the first for years in which Hudson's baneful
presence was not felt, Henry Vincent stood as an advanced radical.
It would be wrong to suggest that all the railwaymen, breathing a
collective sigh of relief, went overwhelmingly into the Vincent camp.
They did not, but many did. In the poll book of 1852 James F.
Masterman and Henry Twentyman, railway guards, appear as
plumpers for Vincent. They would never have dared to do such a
thing at any time that Hudson held the reins of power.

The Hudson era in York was one of corruption and political
oppression, yet the inference from Hudson's adulators' claims seems
to be that in spite of its degrading and corrupt aspects it was in some
way a "golden age ." The Conservatives were in power for a decade
and a half, yet the truth is they did very little of lasting value. Here
it is only fair to say that the powers of local authorities were very
meagre compared with what they were to become in the second half
of the nineteenth century. What *did* happen was that the lines that
made York a great rail centre were either opened or started. The
debate on Hudson, if that is what it is, rests on the claim that *he* made
them all "come to York." The phase in which this is enshrined is
probably apocryphal, but even if it were true—in fairness to Hudson
himself—it ought to be regarded as a declaration of intent, nothing
more, an enthusiastic response by someone excited with a new
project, and flushed with new-found wealth and power. But his
admirers have altered the tense and the sense of his saying—"make"
has become "made" and Hudson is accredited with having *made*

the lines converge on York. This is the Hudson myth as far as York is concerned, and the debate about him has been conducted along the lines of justifying Hitler because he built the autobahns and Mussolini because "he made the trains run on time." But Hudson did *not* make all the lines go to York. He had very little to do with many—nothing to do with most.

In 1850 there were six lines (either built or being built) in and out of York. The York and Scarborough was indisputably Hudson's but it can hardly be called one of the most important. The York, Knaresborough and Harrogate line was the creation of the East and West Yorkshire Junction Company, formed in 1845. The East and West Company was one outside Hudson's control and on its board were no less than five directors of the Leeds, Thirsk, the company that was trying to break Hudson's monopoly on Tees-side; the two were "natural allies" against the Railway King, in fact, who tried to form alliances with the Great North of England-moves which of course, were blocked when Hudson acquired control of the GNE in his fight against the projected London to York line.

The York, Market Weighton, Hull line was not completed when Hudson left York in disgrace, but it *was* his project. However, he could hardly claim it as entirely his own. It was originally projected by Captain Laws, an opponent from the Manchester and Leeds Company Hudson's frantic buying up of land in the East Riding of Yorkshire, in fact, was part of a successful attempt to stop Laws and his companies breaching his monopoly. Having done so, Hudson then built the line himself.

Under construction in 1850 was the line which, in the last resort, was the most important of all running into York. This was the London to York (the Great Northern), the line which Hudson had spent huge sums on trying to stop. What York's history might have been had Hudson succeeded in stopping the line through Peterborough and Doncaster it is useless to speculate, but certainly it would not have had the prosperity or the importance the line gave it. Citizens of York have cause to be pleased that Hudson's efforts were thwarted. Had they been successful, he and his lackeys on the council who petitioned at his bidding, might have been regarded as the great spoilers of the city's destiny.

Almost certainly the line that really did most to make York a great railway centre was the Great North of England. This linked up with York's first line, which, in turn, connected with the system through the Midlands to London. Hudson eventually gained control of the Great North of England, but he had absolutely nothing to do with its creation. This was the result of the efforts of the Quaker businessmen of the Stockton and Darlington Company. R. S. Lambert credits Hudson with great foresight and suggests tha the knew what would happen. Originally he had failed to persuade George Stephenson to terminate his North Midland at York and had persuaded his colleagues that their tiny railway should instead "connect up with Stephenson's new line somewhere about Normanton," Having done this, he knew the northerners would go to York. If Lambert was correct in his contentions then Hudson must certainly be given every credit, for giving his city a brighter future as a railway centre. But he was not correct.

The last of the lines is the original York and North Midland and here it is certainly not true that Hudson is entitled to the credit for its creation. Certainly, when it got under construction he was a guiding light, but James Meek and others of York's business community were responsible for the original conception and they were acting strictly in the way the city's businessmen had acted for many years. York was in the doldrums. It needed cheap coal they reckoned, and it was inevitable that they would become supporters of any new method of transport that seemed likely to produce cheap coal. That was what they, and Hudson, had in mind at that meeting at Tomlinson's Hotel in 1833. Cheap coal, not some grand scheme to reinvigorate York as a railway centre, was their aim. Samuel Smiles recorded that Robert Stephenson, no less, described Hudson's and the others' ambition at this time as "extremely moderate ... most honourable and praiseworthy." The rest came later. Lambert credited Hudson with foresight that he and his colleagues, bent on making York another Bradford, certainly did not have. Many years after he fell, his old friend, Henry Newton, wrote some notes on the originators of the York and North Midland. The notes were not for publication and the need for him to disengage himself from Hudson had gone. It is interesting to note that the people he gave most credit to (apart from himself) were Edward Pease, Stephenson, Samuel Tuke and James Meek.

So Hudson made some of the railways go to York, and he did his level best to stop another. He may have claims to greatness as a national figure, as an "amalgamator," but these claims, if they are justified, have to be set against the part he played personally in creating the railway mania of the '40s. His contribution can never be measured, of course, but it must have been immense. His freebooting style, his outrageous promises and shady methods of financing his projects, led to exaggerated expectations among his own followers and among the railway speculators in general.

Whatever claims Hudson may have as a national figure, however, he has been accredited with achievements as a York personality when bad rule was commonplace—but the extent of corruption and chicanery in York was enormous even by the standards of his own time. During his rule there occurred some of the most degrading incidents in the city's modern history—even if the railways did start their operations.

Part Two

"His Steam Majesty"

RAILWAY MAP OF ENGLAND (A PROPHECY)

HOW differently would the railway system of Britain developed had there been no George Hudson? It is a point of fundamental importance in assessing the credit and debit values of Hudson's self-appointed railway omnipotency. Did his allegedly far-seeing vision create unified rail networks of a more advanced concept than anything his contemporaries could have achieved? Or did his weakness for self-aggrandisement retard worthwhile schemes at the expense of his own whims?

When in doubt, many biographers have an innate tendency to credit rather than discredit their subjects with achievements. Thus, the impression has grown up that Hudson was the architect of the East Coast route. He was not. It was George Stephenson, the "father of railways", who conceived the idea of a trunk line from London to Scotland by way of Rugby, the industrial Midlands, Derby, Leeds, Darlington and Newcastle. Stephenson adopted such a route because of his philosophy of "minerals not men," arguing that it would be more economically sound than a direct line through the then largely agricultural eastern counties.

The "father of railways" was already firmly committed to this plan when he had his famous chance meeting with Hudson at Whitby in the summer of 1834. This was at a time when the success of the Liverpool & Manchester Railway, coupled with a national recovery from the effects of the 1832 Reform Act, was leading to an expression of confidence which culminated in the so-called "little railway mania" of 1836. Plans were afoot to extend the Whitby & Pickering Railway to York, Hudson was closely involved with the embryo York & North Midland Railway and rival factions were advocating direct London–York lines. The cathedral city seemed destined to be enmeshed in a web of iron rails, and Hudson tried to persuade Stephenson that it would be a more logical pivot than Leeds for his visionary trunk route. But, again contrary to what is sometimes stated, he was not successful.

Stephenson held fast to his ideal, and by the autumn of 1835 had completed his detailed plans for what in the following year were to become the Midland Counties and North Midland railways, stretching from a junction with the London & Birmingham Railway at Rugby to Leeds. The North Midland Railway envisaged continuing the Stephenson plan with an extension from Leeds to Newcastle, but was outmanoeuvred. A group of Quakers, headed by Joseph Pease of Darlington, resolved to repeat the success they had already achieved with their pioneering Stockton & Darlington Railway of 1825. They projected the Great North of England Railway for the purpose of "connecting Leeds and York with Newcastle-upon-Tyne and forming a continuation of all the proposed lines from the metropolis towards Scotland."

Thus, the Great North of England started off equally disposed towards Leeds and York, but it was the Central Provisional Com-

mittee of this company that in the end opted for a main line to
York and a branch to Leeds. The branch concept ultimately succumbed to the independent Leeds &Thirsk Railway. Hudson lobbeyed the
Committee on behalf of the York & North Midland Railway,
but personally played no part in the decision which more than anything else was to make railways come to York.

Had there been no Hudson it is possible that, at least at this
stage, there would also have been no York & North Midland
Railway seeking parliamentary sanction to link the city with the
North Midland Railway at Normanton. This was in itself a compromise. To Hudson a feeder route to a trunk line was the next
best thing to an actual trunk railway, while Stephenson, who agreed
to be engineer, felt that he was serving two key northern cities without deviating from his original plan. Without Hudson the Y&NM
might instead have materialised as the York–Leeds line which
George Rennie had recommended in 1834. But in any case, the
Y&NM was not the sole line which the Great North of England
Committee had to consider in deciding between Leeds and York. By
this time the schemes for direct London–York lines had been shelved,
but it was clearly apparent that at some stage the Eastern Counties
would be opened up by rail. And in this respect, York was far
better placed than Leeds.

Hudson's influence on York's early and key railway development
is thus extremely tentative. His planning was dominated on the one
side by Stephenson and on the other by Joseph Pease, and therefore
his achievements at this stage could not be anything but limited. The
most one can say is that he helped to create the York & North
Midland which partially influenced the Great North of England to
focus its southern sights on York. But one cannot go as far as to
state that it was the Y&NM alone which made the Darlington
Quakers turn their backs on Leeds. There is therefore no truth in the
sweeping ascertation that it was Hudson who made the Great
North of England come to York.

The first Hudson annexation was that of the Leeds & Selby
Railway in 1840. It set the pattern for much that was to follow. By
this time the Y&NM had been opened through to its junction with
the North Midland near Normanton, thus not only linking York
with London but also providing a second railway route from Leeds
to York and Leeds to Hull. This last was by means of the Hull &
Selby Railway which was also opened in the same year. Both were in
competition with the earlier and $4\frac{1}{2}$ miles shorter link provided by
the Leeds & Selby line, and Hudson perceived that the competition
could prove disastrous. The L&S was in a weak position as a result
of long-standing trade rivalry with the Aire & Calder Navigation,
and had hardly any alternative but to accept Hudson's offer of a
lease. Yet its directors probably did not foresee Hudson's immediate
and ruthless step which was to close the L&S to passenger traffic

west of Milford Junction the point where it was joined by the Y&NM.

Competition was thus eliminated at a stroke, but—as with many of Hudson's actions—the negative effects were considerable. The Hudson route to York became hopelessly congested, journeys in 1841 often taking as long as two hours. There was the deepest resentment in Leeds, while Hull passengers now had to suffer seemingly interminable waits in changing at bleak Milford Junction. In 1879 G. G. McTurk wrote:

> The older inhabitants of Hull can well remember the horrors of Milford Junction. Waiting for an unknown and indefinite time in a bleak and unprotected station, without proper conveniences, they were kept there until every train for everywhere else had arrived and departed, and then a porter shouted as if in derision, "*Now* for Hull."

It was natural that Hudson should try to gain control of the Hull & Selby Railway at the same time as the L&S, but in this case the directors felt they had a profitable monopoly to exploit and stood out. In retaliation, Hudson used his own funds to buy the steam-tug service between Hull and Selby which had in theory been rendered redundant by the coming of the railway. This he reinstated, but it was a portent of things to come that in 1842 it was operating on a ratio of expenditure to receipts of 52%, compared with the national average of 43%.

But for Hudson it seems likely that both the Leeds & Selby and Hull & Selby lines would ultimately have been absorbed into the Manchester & Leeds Railway. This company evolved from schemes for linking the two ports of Liverpool and Hull by rail, and it would certainly have been better for both Leeds and Hull if it had acquired the lines connecting these latter two centres. From January 1st, 1844, it did indeed enter into a friendly alliance with the H&S, which it was intended would ultimately lead to a partnership. But Hudson regarded this as "a consummation devoutly not to be wished," and so made the H&S shareholders an outstandingly attractive offer for a lease which they accepted against the wishes of their directors.

Thwarted but not totally rebuffed, the Manchester & Leeds now made another bid for Hull. In the first place in 1845 it backed a nominally independent Leeds & York Railway, which Hudson dismissed as "a mere bubble, a perfect absurdity, not worth notice." Yet he put on two non-stop "expresses" over his own in direct Leeds–York route via Castleford, and also through the Y&NM promoted a direct line between the two centres. This was authorised on June 26th, 1846, and even got as far as building a magnificent viaduct over the Wharfe at Tadcaster. The line was abandoned on Hudson's downfall, the viaduct remaining to this day as a lasting monument to his extravagant policies.

The second stage of the Manchester & Leeds bid was a continuation of the Leeds & York line in the form of the York, Hull' East & West Yorkshire Railway. It was here that Hudson made one of his most dramatic moves by buying the 12,000 acre Londes-borough estate from the 6th Duke of Devonshire for £470,000. This blocked all possible routes which his adversary might take, and at the same time provided the "railway king" with a setting for a country seat of suitable magnificence. When his own York–Market Weighton line was opened in October 1847 he erected a private station at the tip of the park, but the implication by Lambert that he also planted an avenue of trees leading up to the house is not correct. This avenue is clearly shown in the 1845 sale plans, and forms a half-completed aristocratic concept for aiding social inter-course between Londesborough Park and neighbouring Everingham Hall.

Thus, the Manchester & Leeds—which became the Lancashire & Yorkshire Railway in 1847—might have extended not only to Hull but also to York had it not been for Hudson. As it was, services between Leeds and York sunk to such a low level that stage coaches were re-introduced between the two towns. On Hudson's fall, the Y&NM Committee of Investigation criticised his closure of the Leeds & Selby Railway west of Milford Junction and recommended that passenger services be reinstated. This was done, but only for local traffic. It was not until as late as April 1869 that the Hudson legacy of inconvenience was finally dispelled by the construction of a cut-off from Church Fenton to Micklefield and a new line from the former L&S terminus at Marsh Lane to the centre of Leeds. The "great-way-round" via Castleford ceased, and Hull passengers no longer had to endure the horrors of Milford Junction.

South of York, Hudson's first major involvement was with the North Midland Railway. By 1842 this line was in serious diffi-culties, partially owing to the colosal £3¼ million spent on con-struction as a result in significant measure of Stephenson's insistence on a ruling gradient no steeper than 1 in 330. Hudson blandished his way into taking charge of a Committee of Inquiry, and proposed to cut working expenses from £44,000 to £27,000 per annum. This extreme measure led to a showdown at the meeting called to re-ceive the report and, with six of the directors resigning, Hudson found himself virtually in charge of the company.

He proceeded to institute his reforms by immediately reducing staff wages and salaries, and not without reason several drivers and firemen voiced strong objections. They received a Hudsonian Christmas present by being paid off on Christmas Eve without notice! Unqualified men and boys were hurriedly recruited in their place, but this did not prevent the onset of the most appalling traffic chaos. Matters came to a head on January 6th, 1843:—

The 3.15 train out of Derby broke down, and was taken into Leeds by the

pilot engine; one hour fifty minutes late. An engine driver proceeded immediately after a train full of passengers, overtook it, and pushed it before him
just as he thought proper. The passenger train which leaves Leeds at 5.30 pm
was standing at Barnsley Station when Edward Jenkins, driver of a luggage
train, ran into it. The usual signals had been given to Jenkins, but from some
cause or other were not observed. There were only three carriages in the
passenger train, and fortunately only one passenger. The carriages were all
smashed to pieces, the head of the unfortunate passenger was completely
cut off.

At the inquest it was revealed that Jenkins had only had three
weeks experience as a driver. The result was a public outcry and the
Board of Trade compelled Hudson to restore the North Midland to
its former state of relative efficiency. Yet it was not the first time nor
the last that the Railway King was to be accused of reducing
working expenses to such an extent that life was endangered. On the
Y&NM on November 11th, 1840, two passengers were killed when
their train was ran into by a goods train driven by an elderly man
with defective sight. Much more serious was a collision near Romford
on the Eastern Counties Railway on July 18th, 1846. The company
was blamed for appointing "incompetent servants," and *Punch*
petitioned Hudson to the effect that

> by reason of the misconduct, negligence, and insobriety of drivers and sundry
> stokers, engineers, policemen, and others, your Majesty's subjects, various
> and several collisions, explosions, and oversettings are continually taking
> place on the Railways, Your Majesty's dominions.

In his first half-year of command, Hudson succeeded in cutting
the North Midlands' working expenses by £11,530. Similarly, the
first month of the united Midland Railway showed an increase in
receipts of £2,500. These were impressive figures but, like so many of
Hudson's achievements, they have to be assessed in the light of the
circumstances which created them.

The amalgamation of the North Midland, Midland Counties and
Birmingham and Derby Junction companies to form the Midland
system represents the first large scale unification of railways. It was
forced through by Hudson in 1843, despite intense opposition from
the Midland Counties chairman. Undoubtedly this, and the other
Hudson amalgamations and absorptions, helped to achieve better
results than would have been the case if the respective lines had
stayed independent. But the real question is: without Hudson,
would such amalgamations in any case have ultimately taken place?
In most instances it is arguable that they would, either during the
"railway mania" of 1845-7 or, more likely, in the ensuing financial
crisis which tended to create a policy of join forces or bust. The two
southern constituents of the Midland had become impoverished
through ruinous fare-cutting, and it is likely that sooner or later
they would themselves have amalgamated or would have been
absorbed into a larger company such as the London & North

Western Railway. Similarly, if the Birmingham–Gloucester–Bristol line had not been captured by the Hudson empire it would almost certainly still have become part of a major network—that of the Great Western.

The *cause celebre* of Midland affairs at this time was the tiny Leeds & Bradford Railway. Hudson took a leading role in promoting this independent company in the autumn of 1843, and himself put his name down for 600 of the £50 shares. He allotted others to his friends in York, and in a few weeks the premium on his own shares amounted to no less than £6,000. North Midland shareholders were understandably incensed, for the L&B was a natural extension of their line. There was further trouble during the height of the "railway mania" when it became obvious that the L&B was too small to remain independent. Hudson appeared to agree to an amalgamation with the Manchester & Leeds, then desperately anxious to make up for its missed oportunities of the past and obtain its own line into Leeds. But in view of the acrimony between the two, one is bound to wonder if this was an error of judgement or a cunning prelude for what was to follow. For at the last moment the L&B switched its allegiance to the Midland.

Hudson, although chairman of both companies, was brazen enough to attend the meeting called on July 25th, 1846, to ratify the purchase. He even went to the dictatorial lengths of proposing a lease at a high rate of 10% for 999 years, and thus could only blame himself for the ensuing outburst with cries such as "You are buyer and seller too" being bandied around the room. It was this incident which precipitated the first investigation into Hudson's methods of accounting, and has often been seen as marking the beginning of his downfall. The doubts among the shareholders were well founded, for it was later proved that the liabilities of the L&B were £110,000 and its assets a mere £261, while John Waddington—its deputy chairman—had made a personal profit out of the line of £62,500. As with many other Hudson lines, it was a long time before the L&B fully recovered from his reign.

North of York, Hudson at one stage envisaged a grandiose concept for extending the Midland Railway right through to Scotland via the Y&NM. This was in effect adopting Stephenson's plan, with a deviation to serve York, but the government of the day refused to authorise the £2 million required. Hudson therefore turned his attention to building an extension of the Great North of England Railway which, owing to the financial difficulties of the late 1830s and early 1840s, had been advised by Robert Stephenson to limit construction to a line from York to Darlington. The Railway King's brave scheme for unifying existing lines to help to extend railway communications to Gateshead was undoubtedly one of his finest achievements, although a Darlington critic denounced it as "an abortion, with a crooked back and a crooked snout, conceived in cupidity and begotten in fraud."

Again though, one must ask if such unification would in any event have taken place, and again it is arguable that Hudson simply gave the inevitable a headstart. Here too the good work was nullified by extravagance. At the Gateshead terminus Hudson got his architect, G. T. Andrews of York, to design the ostentatious Greenesfield station with its 352 feet long ionic front, elaborate facilities and adjoining hotel. Yet the haste for exuberant display was such that the station was built before plans for the high level bridge over the Tyne into Newcastle were finalised. The two were at variance, and when the bridge was erected the station was left on a dead-end spur and closed after a life of only six years.

Hudson's Newcastle & Darlington Junction Railway absorbed a large number of small lines in County Durham, and made its major step in 1845 when it took over the Great North of England on terms which the chairman felt "would be absolute madness any longer to resist." Hudson admitted that he was paying more than the line was worth, but publicly justified his actions on the familiar grounds that a unified railway between York and Newcastle would reduce working expenses.

But, as was so often the case, there was another underlying reason. From the outset the Great North of England had hoped that one day its line would be linked at York with a direct route to London, and now just such a line was being promoted. The London & York Railway was the worst threat which Hudson had yet faced, for if it was successful the Midland would cease to be a trunk route to the north. His reactions were therefore characteristically extreme. In the first place he bullied a special meeting of Midland shareholders into sanctioning the raising of £2½ million of new capital for building lines into intended London & York territory. His next move was to obstruct the passage of his opponents' Bill in any way possible, although the oft-repeated statement that he employed counsel at a daily expense of £3,000 is not correct. But by the most devious tactics he did manage to spread the committee proceedings over no fewer than 70 days before descending to methods of near-criminality in order to have the Bill thrown out in the Lords.

Realising that he might not be so successful in the following year, Hudson now decided to move his base from York to London in order to take over the chairmanship of the Eastern Counties Railway. He felt that he might be able to transform this ailing and meandering system into a direct rival to the London & York, although his first and more sensible action was to try and amalgamate the two. When this failed there was no alternative but another round of Parliamentary opposition, which this time culminated in the new company receiving the royal assent as the Great Northern Railway on June 26th, 1846. The price it had had to pay in legal expenses and the like in order to repel Hudson was a colossal

£500,000. The "railway king" was faced with a bill of £100,000, and in addition he spent £15,000 on acquiring Albert Gate—one of the most splendid mansions in London— and £14,000 on furnishing it. A side move was his insistence that the Eastern Counties should construct a virtually isolated railway from Huntingdon to St. Ives in order to block any Great Northern designs in this direction. This $4\frac{3}{4}$ mile line cost a fantastic £130,000 per mile, although for a time it was worked merely by a horse tram.

It is one of the gravest charges against Hudson that money was frittered away on this scale in the name of self-interest. In this case it achieved nothing. Hudson was left with the Midland Railway which had no future as a trunk route to Scotland, and the Eastern Counties which even he must have realised was not a viable alternative line to the North. He therefore resorted to treachery. One year after the incorporation of the Great Northern he smuggled through Parliament almost unnoticed a short line for linking Burton Salmon to Knottingley. Its ostensible purpose could hardly have been more innocent: to obtain lime in the area and link the local population with Leeds and Hull. Yet this short spur provided a means by which the Great Northern could use the Y&NM to gain access to York, and thus be spared the expense of building its own line north of Doncaster.

It was a skilled, and in many ways praiseworthy attempt by Hudson to rid himself of the Midland and Eastern Counties, and retain the companies centred on York as well as control of the northern half of the East Coast Route. But, like the Leeds & Bradford lease, it was to sow seeds of doubt in the eyes of Midland shareholders which culminated in a demand for his resignation. This coincided with wholesale revelations of his financial malpractices on other lines, and brought perhaps the most painful downfall any "monarch" has ever suffered.

A fully balanced judgement of Hudson is virtually impossible to achieve. It has already been shown that he did not make all railways come to York. And it seems wrong to describe a man who used such obstructive tactics for his own ends as a great architect of the present-day railway system. Perhaps the best that can be said is that he was ahead of the crowd and gave what were to become the Midland and North Eastern Railways such a head-start that they remained pre-eminent into the 20th century. But Hudson achieved this head-start by laying the foundations of these lines in the impoverished early 1840s, and only did so by the use of financial methods which today would be regarded as criminal. In other words, he achieved a certain measure of success by much malpractice and massive squandering of money. Those who now regard him as a master railway strategist might do worse than ponder on the thousands of hapless individuals who became almost penurious as a result of his despicable financial policies.

The reign of King Hudson

1836

Appointed first chairman of York & North Midland Railway, authorised June 21st, 1836, to build line from York to junction with North Midland Railway at Normanton.

1839

May 29th: Y&NM opened from York to junction with Leeds & Selby Railway.

1840

July 1st: Y&NM opened throughout, placing York in reasonably direct railway communication with London.

November 9th: To eliminate competition, Y&NM leases Leeds & Selby Railway (the first line in the West Riding when opened on September 22nd, 1834).

1841

Hudson elected chairman of Newcastle & Darlington Junction Railway, authorised June 18th, 1842, and superseding the abandoned portion of the Great North of England Railway north of Darlington. The N&DJ was a new line from Darlington to Rainton Meadows with running powers thence to Gateshead over the Durham Junction Railway (authorised June 16th, 1834; opened August 24th, 1838); the Brandling Junction Railway (authorised July 21st, 1835; first portion opened January 15th, 1839); and the Pontop & South Shields Railway (incorporated May 23rd, 1842, taking over the northern portion of the Stanhope & Tyne Railway, opened 1834).

1842

November: Becomes effectual chairman of North Midland Railway (authorised 1836 and opened July 1st, 1840, Derby to Leeds).

1844

February: N&DJ takes determinable lease of Newcastle & Berwick Railway so as to float company. Hudson first chairman of new company.

April 15th: First portion of N&DJ opened.

May 10th: Royal assent given to first large scale railway amalgamation, the Birmingham & Derby Junction Railway (authorised 1836, opened 1839 Hampton–Derby), the Midland Counties Railway (authorised 1836, opened 1840 Rugby–Derby) and the North Midland Railway combining to form the Midland Railway. Hudson architect of the scheme and first chairman of the new company.

May 23rd: Purchase of Leeds & Selby Railway by Y&NM authorised.

May 23rd: Construction of high level bridge over Tyne by N&DJ and N&B authorised.

May 23rd: Purchase of Durham Junction Railway by N&DJ authorised.

June 19th: N&DJ opened throughout, completing railway communication from London to Gateshead.

August 13th: Purchase of Brandling Junction Railway by N&DJ agreed.

November: Newcastle & North Shields Railway (authorised June 21st, 1836; opened June 18th, 1839) provisionally amalgamated with N&B. Amalgamation authorised 1845 and effective from July 1846.

1845

February 8th: Midland leases Birmingham & Gloucester Railway (authorised April 22nd, 1836; opened throughout August 17th, 1841) and Bristol & Gloucester Railway (authorised 1839; opened as broad gauge line July 8th, 1844). Hudson empire now extends from Bristol to Gateshead.

June 30th: Purchase authorised of Whitby & Pickering Railway by Y&NM (hitherto isolated horse-worked line authorised May 6th, 1833; opened throughout May 26th, 1836).

July 1st: Y&NM leases Hull & Selby Railway (authorised June 21st, 1836; opened July 2nd, 1840).

July 1st: N&DJ begins working Great North of England Railway (authorised July 4th, 1836, Darlington–Newcastle; July 12th, 1837, York–Darlington. Southern portion opened March 30th, 1841). The GNE had been leased in May 1845 by the Midland, Y&NM and N&DJ so as to give Hudson control of the whole of the East Coast route from Rugby to Berwick.

July 4th: Purchase of Erewash Valley Railway by Midland authorised.

July 8th: Y&NM lines from York to Scarborough and Pickering opened (had been authorised July 4th, 1844).

July: 21st Purchase of Sheffield & Rotherham Railway by Midland authorised.

September: Hudson purchases the 12,000 acre Londesborough Park estate from the Duke of Devonshire for £470,000, partially to block competing lines between York and Hull.

October 13th: Appointed chairman of the Eastern Counties Railway, then main line from London to Brandon where joined Norfolk Railway extending to Norwich. Hudson proposes that Eastern Counties should form trunk route to north via Lincoln.

October 25th: Manchester & Leeds Railway admitted by Y&NM as joint lessee of Hull & Selby Railway (although lease never in fact completed).

1846

June 26th: Incorporation of Great Northern Railway (London–Doncaster) splits Hudson kingdom into two portions.

July: Midland absorbs Leicester & Swannington Railway (the oldest constituent company of the Midland).

July: Midland leases Leeds & Bradford Railway (incorporated 1844 with Hudson as chairman; opened July 1st, 1846). Lease of one

Hudson company to another at an excessive figure initiated an enquiry into his practices.

July 27th: N&DJ purchases Great North of England Railway. Combined companies become York & Newcastle Railway.

August 4th: Midland line from Nottingham to Lincoln opened.

September 2nd: Opening of Midland Syston–Peterborough line as far as Melton Mowbray.

September 11th: Y&N Richmond branch opened (authorised by GNE Act July 21st, 1845).

October 2nd: Opening of Stamford–Peterborough section of Midland Syston–Peterborough line.

October 5th: Opening of Y&NM Seamer–Filey line.

October 6th: Opening of Y&NM Hull–Bridlington line (authorised by Hull & Selby Railway Act, June 30th, 1845).

October 12th: Y&N takes over Hartlepool Dock & Railway (authorised June 1st, 1832; opened November 23rd, 1835). Lease not actually sanctioned until July 22nd, 1848).

1847

January 1st: Y&N absorbs Durham & Sunderland Railway (authorised August 13th, 1834; first section formally opened August 30th, 1836).

January 14th: Eastern Counties Railway opened Ely North Junction –Peterborough.

March 1st: First portion of Newcastle & Berwick Railway opened.

March 16th: Extension of Leeds & Bradford Railway to Keighley opened.

May 3rd: Eastern Counties Railway opened March–Wisbech.

June 17th: Y&N branch Pilmoor–Boroughbridge opened.

July 1st: Whitby & Pickering Railway opened to locomotive traffic.

July 1st: Opening of Newcastle–Tweedmouth section of Newcastle & Berwick Railway completes East Coast route from London to Edinburgh with the exception of the high-level bridges over the Tyne and Tweed.

August 9th: Amalgamation authorised of Y&N and Newcastle & Berwick Railway to form York, Newcastle & Berwick Railway.

August 10th: Y&NM Church Fenton-Harrogate line opened as far as Spofforth.

August 17th: Eastern Counties Railway opened Cambridge–St. Ives.

September 8th: Extension of Leeds & Bradford Railway to Skipton opened.

October 4th: Y&NM York–Market Weighton line opened.

October 20th: Opening of Y&NM Bridlington–Filey line completes rail link from Hull to Scarborough.

1848

February 1st: Eastern Counties Railway opened St. Ives–March.

March 6th: YN&B Northallerton–Bedale branch opened as far as Leeming (authorised June 26th, 1846).

March 20th: Opening of Melton Mowbray–Stamford line completes Midland's Syston–Peterborough route.

May: Eastern Counties Railway commences to work Norfolk Railway.

May 8th: Y&NM Hull Paragon station opened.

July 20th: Y&NM Spofforth–Harrogate section opened.

July 22nd: Parliament sanctions leasing by YN&B of the Great North of England, Clarence & Hartlepool Junction Railway (authorised July 3rd, 1837; first portion opened March 18th, 1839). This line had in fact been leased by the Y&N in October 1846.

August: YN&B takes control of West Durham Railway (portion opened as wayleave line June 12th, 1839; authorised July 4th, 1839).

August 1st: Y&NM Selby–Market Weighton line opened.

August 1st: On behalf of YN&B, Hudson leases Newcastle & Carlisle Railway (authorised May 22nd, 1829; opened throughout June 18th, 1838). Lease never ratified.

August 29th: Opening of temporary high-level bridge over Tyne.

October: Eastern Counties Railway leases Newmarket Railway (opened Chesterford–Newmarket March 19th, 1848).

October 1st: On behalf of YN&B, Hudson leases Maryport & Carlisle Railway (authorised 1837; opened throughout February 10th, 1845). Lease never ratified.

October 2nd: Midland lines opened: Coalville–Burton; Nottingham–Kirkby; Skipton–Colne.

October 2nd: Eastern Counties Railway opened Maldon–Braintree.

October 30th: Opening of East & West Yorkshire Junction Railway (York–Knaresborough; authorised July 16th, 1846). Worked by YN&B.

November: Hudson reaches agreement to lease Stockton & Darlington Railway to YN&B. Not put into effect.

1849

February 20th: Half-yearly meeting of YN&B appoints Committee of Investigation to look into Hudson's share transactions.

February 28th: Hudson resigns from chairmanship of Eastern Counties Railway. Committee of Investigation appointed.

March 20th: Meeting of Midland Railway's Liverpool shareholders calls for Hudson's resignation.

April: Hudson incriminated by reports of YN&B and Eastern Counties' investigating committees.

April 19th: Resigns chairmanship of Midland Railway. Committee of Investigation appointed.

May 4th: Resigns chairmanship of YN&B. Further Committee of Inquiry appointed.

May 17th: An unlucky thirteen years of railway sovereignty ends with Hudson's resignation as chairman of the Y&NM.